May–August 2020

Day by Day
with
God

Rooting women's lives in the Bible

The Bible Reading Fellowship
15 The Chambers, Vineyard
Abingdon OX14 3FE
brf.org.uk

The Bible Reading Fellowship (BRF) is a Registered Charity (233280)

ISBN 978 0 85746 912 0
All rights reserved

This edition © 2020 The Bible Reading Fellowship
Cover image © Thinkstock

Distributed in Australia by:
MediaCom Education Inc, PO Box 610, Unley, SA 5061
Tel: 1 800 811 311 | admin@mediacom.org.au

Distributed in New Zealand by:
Scripture Union Wholesale, PO Box 760, Wellington
Tel: 04 385 0421 | suwholesale@clear.net.nz

Acknowledgements
Scripture quotations marked with the following acronyms are taken from the version shown.
Where no acronym is given, the quotation is taken from the same version as the headline
reference. NIV: The Holy Bible, New International Version (Anglicised edition) copyright ©
1979, 1984, 2011 by Biblica. Used by permission of Hodder & Stoughton Publishers, a Hachette
UK company. All rights reserved. 'NIV' is a registered trademark of Biblica. UK trademark
number 1448790. KJV: The Authorised Version of the Bible (The King James Bible), the rights
in which are vested in the Crown, are reproduced by permission of the Crown's Patentee,
Cambridge University Press. NLT: The Holy Bible, New Living Translation, copyright © 1996,
2004, 2007, 2013. Used by permission of Tyndale House Publishers, Inc., Carol Stream, Illinois
60188. All rights reserved. AMPC: The Amplified® Bible (AMPC), Copyright © 1954, 1958,
1962, 1964, 1965, 1987 by The Lockman Foundation. Used by permission. www.Lockman.
org. MSG: The Message, copyright © 1993, 1994, 1995, 1996, 2000, 2001, 2002 by Eugene H.
Peterson. Used by permission of NavPress. All rights reserved. Represented by Tyndale House
Publishers, Inc. SOU: The Source: With Extensive Notes on Greek Word Meaning. Copyright ©
2004 by Ann Nyland. Used by permission of Smith and Stirling Publishers. All rights reserved.
TPT: The Passion Translation®. Copyright © 2017 by BroadStreet Publishing® Group, LLC. Used
by permission. All rights reserved. thePassionTranslation.com. ESV: The Holy Bible, English
Standard Version, published by HarperCollins Publishers, © 2001 Crossway Bibles, a division
of Good News Publishers. Used by permission. All rights reserved. AMP: The Amplified® Bible
(AMP), Copyright © 2015 by The Lockman Foundation. Used by permission. www.Lockman.
org. CEV: The Contemporary English Version. New Testament © American Bible Society 1991,
1992, 1995. Old Testament © American Bible Society 1995. Anglicisations © British & Foreign
Bible Society 1996. Used by permission.

Every effort has been made to trace and contact copyright owners for material used in
this resource. We apologise for any inadvertent omissions or errors, and would ask those
concerned to contact us so that full acknowledgement can be made in the future.

A catalogue record for this book is available from the British Library

Printed by Gutenberg Press, Tarxien, Malta

Day by Day
with
God

Edited by **Jill Rattle**

May–August 2020

Writers in this issue

Nell Goddard is a writer at the London Institute for Contemporary Christianity and author of *Musings of a Clergy Child: Growing into a faith of my own* (BRF, 2017).

Jennifer Rees Larcombe runs Beauty from Ashes, an organisation that supports people adjusting to bereavement and trauma. She lives in rural Kent and loves gardening and entertaining her 15 grandchildren.

Tracy Williamson lives in Kent, sharing a home with her friend and ministry partner Marilyn Baker and their two assistance dogs. Tracy has written several books, her latest being *The Father's Kiss* (Authentic Media, 2018).

Michele D. Morrison, a graduate in English literature, has worked in public relations, edited an environmental technology magazine and published many articles, prayers and Bible studies.

Hannah Fytche read theology at the University of Cambridge and now works at St Andrew's Church in Chesterton. She's passionate about seeing God's love transform lives and communities, and she embraces this passion through writing, speaking and spending time with friends and family.

Chris Leonard lives in Surrey with her husband. They have three young grandchildren and Chris remains busy leading creative writing workshops and holidays. She is the author of 21 books. **chrisleonardwriting.uk**

Lyndall Bywater is a freelance writer, trainer and consultant in all things prayer. She has a passion to help people get to know God better and is the author of two BRF books, *Faith in the Making* and *Prayer in the Making*.

Annie Willmot is an author, speaker and funeral pastor. She has a background in children and families ministry but can currently be found writing or chasing her two young children around. **honestconversation.co.uk**

Sheila Jacobs is a writer, editor and award-winning author. She lives in rural north Essex, attends an Elim church, where she serves as a deacon, and is also a day chaplain at a retreat centre.

Caroline Fletcher is a freelance writer. She has an MPhil in biblical studies and trained as an RE teacher. She is married to a vicar and is involved in all-age services and youth work at her church in Sheffield.

Jill Rattle writes...

Welcome to this issue of *Day by Day with God*! The observant reader will have noticed that Ali Herbert's name is no longer linked with mine as co-editor. After three years of study and training, Ali has been ordained into the Church of England and is working as a curate at St Luke's Gas Street, Birmingham, and also as part of the diocesan church-planting team. She needs to release the co-editorship which she has held for a number of years. Do pray with me that the Lord will bless her new ministry with his grace and power.

When I held Ali in my arms as a newborn all those years ago, I was overwhelmed with gratitude to God and began a life's journey of prayer and love for her. To see what God has done in her life is one of my greatest joys.

We both have the privilege of being part of a 'dynasty' of Christian believers. I don't know, of course, but I like to think that many years ago a woman of God began praying into her family and its future generations. Do we underestimate the impact of prayer on years to come? Who are the children in your family or your church's family that you could undertake to pray for – and also for their children? Maybe one glorious day we'll know the impact of our prayers. And how thrilled we will be!

Each reading we have for you in this issue ends with a call to prayer. To pray out of the scriptures is one of the most spiritually powerful things we can do. I urge you to give time to that last little paragraph on each page.

This issue, we're pleased to welcome a new contributor – Annie Willmot, who for a week looks at some of the things Jesus lovingly tells us to do and also not to do. Jesus says if we do what he says, we are like a wise person who builds their house on a rock. In the final set of notes, Caroline Fletcher shows us how the book of Proverbs defines the difference between wisdom and foolishness.

I love how, without my planning, notes from different contributors often complement each other. Hannah Fytche concludes her notes about servanthood by talking about the fruit of the Spirit, beautifully leading into Chris Leonard's unusual set on fruit and fruitfulness.

Enjoy them all!

Hospitality

Nell Goddard writes:

What comes to mind when you consider the word 'hospitality'? For me, it reminds me of Christmas at my parents' house. Operating an open-home policy all year round, we peak at lunchtime on 25 December when anyone in the church who would otherwise be alone is invited for lunch. With anywhere between 11 and 30 guests, it is messy and loud and tiring and glorious, all at the same time.

Perhaps you have been on the receiving end of some remarkable hospitality. Perhaps you have the gift of hospitality yourself. Or perhaps you feel incredibly ill-equipped to be hospitable, and you don't really know where to start.

Over the next nine days, we'll be journeying through some passages in the Bible which talk about hospitality. Although we will consider only nine passages, hospitality plays a big part in biblical ethics – Israelites and early Christians were instructed to practise this virtue, and it was the mark of leaders from Abraham all the way through to the early church. Hospitality is also something which God clearly shows us – his covenant people – throughout the Bible.

Biblical hospitality isn't just about opening up your home and your life to those nearby who are in need (although that's certainly a part of it); it extends far beyond that. As we journey through scripture, we will discover that hospitality takes many forms – it can be financial; it can be offered to complete strangers or dear friends; it can be done in community or through individual acts of faith. We will begin and end, however, by looking at God's hospitality to us, both here on earth and in heaven.

A lot of hospitality in the Bible is centred around food – from Abraham offering a meal to strangers (who turn out to be angels), all the way through to the wedding feast of the Lamb in Revelation. Perhaps, through these studies, you will be inspired to share a meal with someone new.

As we journey through the Bible, reflecting on the many forms of hospitality it not only demonstrates but exhorts us to imitate, my prayer is that we would learn both how we can grow in this gift ourselves *and* how we can bask more fully in the beautiful, eternal, faithful hospitality of God to us, every single day.

God's hospitality to us

You prepare a table before me in the presence of my enemies. You anoint my head with oil; my cup overflows. Surely your goodness and love will follow me all the days of my life, and I will dwell in the house of the Lord forever. (NIV)

Have you ever thrown a banquet? I would guess you probably haven't. Banquets aren't really a thing we do anymore. The closest we get is, perhaps, a wedding breakfast to celebrate a new marriage. Wedding breakfasts will feature later in these studies, but for today we must focus on the slightly alien concept of a banquet and what it can teach us about God's hospitality.

Laying a table for someone was – and still is today – the act of a gracious host. But there's more than that hidden in this psalm's imagery. In the psalmist's world, to dine at someone's table was to create a bond of mutual loyalty. And this is no ordinary banquet; this is a banquet thrown by the Lord, the God of Israel.

The feast is in the presence of 'enemies', suggesting a victory celebration, perhaps with the defeated rivals present as reluctant guests. There's a sense of God's protection and provision, past and present.

The imagery continues with the overflowing cup, symbolising the blessings God has showered upon the psalmist – so much so that he can declare that God's 'goodness and love' will follow him all the days of his life, and that his eternal dwelling place is secure.

We are only scratching the surface here. But we must begin our exploration of hospitality by at least trying to grasp the height, breadth and depth of God's hospitality to us, for it is only out of that knowledge, that reassurance, that we are truly free to act in hospitality to others.

We can stand firm in the knowledge that God's goodness and loving kindness will pursue us, and that our place at his table in his house is secure for eternity. From those truths, we can give of what we have today.

Father, thank you for your gracious and eternal hospitality to us; for the goodness and loving kindness that pursues us all the days of our lives. May the knowledge of your faithfulness inspire me in my own hospitality.

NELL GODDARD

Community hospitality

They sold property and possessions to give to anyone who had need. Every day they continued to meet together in the temple courts. They broke bread in their homes and ate together with glad and sincere hearts, praising God and enjoying the favour of all the people. (NIV)

Which bit of this description of the lives of the early Christians do you find the most challenging? Is it the signs and wonders? How they shared everything? The selling of property? The giving of their possessions to those in need? Their regularly meeting together? Or perhaps that they met together in one another's houses?

The kind of person you are, the kind of upbringing you had and, quite frankly, the kind of day you're having can all influence which you find the most appealing and which you would really rather ignore.

Some of these, however, are difficult no matter how you feel, especially in today's culture. Selling your property in order to give the money away? Although for many people today the very idea of owning our own home is laughable, perhaps even more laughable is the idea that once we've scraped together a deposit and bought a house, we would then sell it if we found a Christian brother or sister in need.

Although they 'broke bread in their homes', suggesting some continuing ownership of property, it is likely that they sold much of their land. This was a significant sacrifice: land was not just an economic asset but a part of their heritage; it was part of what God had promised them.

But they saw that members of their family were in need, and so they made material and economic sacrifices. And they saw many come to know Christ. There is a strange freedom to be found when you stop clinging to material possessions and instead start sharing with those in need.

Hospitality – generosity – looks like laying down material and economic prosperity for the sake of family who are in need, no matter how hard that may be.

Thank you, Father, for the example of the first Christians and their radical hospitality. Please teach me how to give generously from what you have given me, and to share whatever I can with my brothers and sisters in need.

NELL GODDARD

Distinctive hospitality

Be devoted to one another in love. Honour one another above yourselves. Never be lacking in zeal, but keep your spiritual fervour, serving the Lord. Be joyful in hope, patient in affliction, faithful in prayer. Share with the Lord's people who are in need. Practise hospitality. (NIV)

When you read the word 'love', what do you think of? Grand gestures, extravagant gifts, bold declarations? Racing through an airport, writing a message in the sky, crashing a wedding? Disney films and popular romcoms are pretty clear that those are signs of true love.

It's easy to fall into the trap of thinking that 'love' is limited to such simple definitions and straightforward actions. And yet, the subheading for this passage is 'love in action' (NIV), and it is here that we find the beginnings of an answer. Spoiler alert: it doesn't look much like a Disney film.

To love is to help others in their various needs. It is not about feelings, big red hearts or extravagant gestures; it is simply about helping, caring for others and forgiving quickly. It is to bless those who persecute you, to live in harmony with others, to 'be willing to associate with people of low position', perhaps even inviting them into your own home.

Paul is clear that this is how all Christians should act. This is the baseline of what we should be doing for one another. As far as is possible, we should 'live at peace with everyone', being 'joyful in hope, patient in affliction, faithful in prayer'.

As I read this, I almost feel like the grand gestures and extravagant gifts of a Disney film would be easier. Racing through an airport is a one-time thing; honouring others above myself is a lesson it will take a lifetime to learn.

But that is the beauty of learning to love as Jesus taught – it is never just a one-time thing. It is a way of living, a way of being, which changes us as it changes the world around us.

Father, teach me to love well.

NELL GODDARD

Across enemy lines

'You have heard that it was said, "Love your neighbour and hate your enemy." But I tell you, love your enemies and pray for those who persecute you, that you may be children of your Father in heaven.' (NIV)

Would you invite your enemy round for dinner? Someone who had hurt you or a loved one? Someone who was a bully or a manipulator? Someone who had ruined your life, stolen from you or shamed you beyond what you could bear?

I'd guess not. I certainly wouldn't – not out of choice, anyway. The same can be said of those to whom Jesus was originally giving these instructions – they knew the rule of loving neighbour and hating enemy. But Jesus surprises them, just as he surprises us: he tells us, in no uncertain terms, 'Love your enemies and pray for those who persecute you.'

This 'love' isn't to do with a warm fuzzy feeling. It's about what you *do*. 'Love' isn't just a good feeling; it's a way of being, a way of acting, a way of doing things.

So when Jesus tells us to 'love our enemies', we are being instructed to do more than just not hate them. We are being asked to act towards them as we would to our own family.

This is, perhaps, where hospitality feels the hardest. This is not something that can be done in our own human strength – it is only through the work of the Spirit, in the power of God, that we can truly begin to act in this way.

And it is through such acts, such profoundly countercultural ways of doing life, that we begin to not only discover for ourselves but also show to others something of the living God, who loved us and lived this in its entirety – loving so much that he died for those who had rejected him, so that they could become children of his Father in heaven.

Father, please give me the strength to love my enemies. Give me the words to pray for those who have persecuted me and mine. Teach me your ways, O God, for I cannot do this without you.

NELL GODDARD

Costly hospitality

'For this is what the Lord, the God of Israel, says: "The jar of flour will not be used up and the jug of oil will not run dry until the day the Lord sends rain on the land."' (NIV)

'Joey doesn't share food!' It's a classic line from the final season of the sitcom *Friends*, where Joey refuses to share his chips with his date. In a world of plenty, it's a funny reference.

But in a world of scarcity, amidst drought and famine, it is less amusing, and perhaps more understandable. After all, how likely would you be to share your last bit of food, not with a date but with a stranger you met on the road? The widow in this story has planned to make a final meal for herself and her son, and then die from starvation.

She has almost nothing to give… and a stranger asks for everything: her final meal, her final chance to feed her son.

What would you do?

Even for the most generous of people, this is not an easy ask. And the 'Lord, the God of Israel' that Elijah references? The one he promises will look after her? That isn't even her god! Elijah is in the land where Baal was worshipped.

But despite this, the widow has faith. Her simple action of making a loaf first for Elijah suggests that, perhaps, she recognises him as a 'man of God'. She offers him her spare room and feeds him.

From the sharing of her final meal, the last bits of her food, the widow learns of God's miraculous provision to those who are faithful. This becomes even more apparent in the following verses, when Elijah raises her son from the dead.

To share when we have plenty is difficult; to share when we have almost nothing is nearly impossible. May we, too, have the quiet generosity and hope-filled faith of a widow with nothing more than a handful of flour and a little olive oil.

Father, teach me to be generous, not only when I have plenty to spare, but also when I feel I have nothing to give.

NELL GODDARD

Stranger danger?

Do not forget to show hospitality to strangers, for by so doing some people have shown hospitality to angels without knowing it. (NIV)

'Stranger danger!' Don't talk to strangers, and definitely don't get in their cars. These are rules which are embedded into our consciousness from an early age. But, at the same time, we have sayings such as, 'Strangers are just friends you haven't met yet.' Seems like somewhat of a contradiction, doesn't it?

How do we hold in tension these two pieces of secular wisdom? Well, the passage in Hebrews is pretty clear: 'Show hospitality to strangers,' it says. It is possible that the 'some people' who had 'shown hospitality to angels without knowing it' is a reference back to Genesis 18, where Abraham fed three strangers who turned out to be angels of the Lord.

But how do we do this today? It's not straightforward, and it requires wisdom and discernment. We do, of course, have a responsibility to protect vulnerable people living in our homes. The importance of that must not be overlooked. But one of the hallmarks of the early Christian community (see Acts 2:43–47, Saturday 2 May note) was radical hospitality, and that must also be a mark of our own communities today. Part of being in the family of God is to care for one another in practical ways.

What might it look like if we trusted God for our safety and security, listened to the prompts of the Spirit and welcomed in strangers? 'The Lord is my helper; I will not be afraid' (Hebrews 13:6, quoting Psalm 118:6). By welcoming in strangers, we may find ourselves blessed in unexpected ways.

To trust in God is to trust him not only with your eternal salvation, but with your day-to-day life and safety as well – and that of those you love. You may be surprised in the most delightful of ways.

Father, I know that you are good. Thank you that you are trustworthy. Thank you for your provision and your protection. Please show me how I can bless strangers with your love through my hospitality.

NELL GODDARD

Financial hospitality

Even when I was in Thessalonica, you sent me aid more than once when I was in need. Not that I desire your gifts; what I desire is that more be credited to your account. I have received full payment and have more than enough. (NIV)

How far do you think financial generosity and hospitality are linked? Paul is pretty clear in this passage that the two are closely related, as he writes to the church in Philippi to thank them for their generous monetary gifts that helped him when he was 'in need'.

For some, the gift of financial support is easy; for others, it is incredibly costly and requires a great deal of sacrifice. We are not told where the Philippian church fell on this spectrum. What we do know, however, is that they are the only church Paul preached to that continued supporting him financially after he left – although it is unlikely the Philippians were aware of this when they sent the money.

We never know what impact our financial generosity – our hospitality with money – may have on someone's life, faith or ministry. Paul makes clear early on that he did not 'desire your gifts', but his delight comes from their faith finding a practical outworking.

This wasn't about the Philippians earning their salvation; it was a reflection of their deep trust in God to provide for them. Paul can therefore promise the Philippians what he had learnt throughout his ministry – that God will supply their needs in all circumstances, too.

This presents a challenge to us in our daily lives: how is our faith, our deep trust in God and his provision, working itself out in how we use our money? How is it working itself out in how we are hospitable and to whom we are generous?

Generosity – and particularly financial generosity – looks different for each of us. But it all flows out of our trust in God and is rooted in the prayer that we, like Paul, would learn to 'be content whatever the circumstances'.

Father, please teach me contentment, and help me to be generous with whatever it is that I have. May I hold my money lightly and trust you for provision in every situation.

NELL GODDARD

Hospitality to foreigners

'Do not ill-treat or oppress a foreigner, for you were foreigners in Egypt.' (NIV)

Have you even been in a foreign country and felt somewhat out of your depth? The language barrier and the fear of making a cultural faux pas and inadvertently offending someone can be two particularly difficult parts of visiting another country.

These fears are no doubt exacerbated many times over when you are not just visiting but moving there. Moreover, if you do not understand the language or the subtle cultural cues, you are much more open to exploitation. There are plenty of stories of such incidents in our world today.

This was even more the case in Old Testament times, when there wasn't Google Translate to help with the language barrier, nor the Universal Declaration of Human Rights to appeal to when exploitation occurred.

Throughout Exodus 22, we see God's desire that his people take care of those who are helpless, disadvantaged, vulnerable or at risk of exploitation, particularly widows, orphans and foreigners. It is a sign of God's people that they care for those the world forgets or takes advantage of. God is clear that his people must not be guilty of exploitation of others – no matter how 'different' they might be.

We may not personally have experienced being a foreigner in a strange land – at least not for longer than a few weeks' holiday. Perhaps we cannot empathise as well as the Israelites, having been slaves in Egypt, could, but that does not change how we, as the people of God, are instructed to treat those who are strangers or foreigners today. We must care for the disadvantaged and the vulnerable – offer them hospitality, perhaps teach them our language, instruct them in our culture and welcome them in as far as we can.

Father, help me to be hospitable to everyone, even those with whom communication is difficult. Please protect those in foreign lands from exploitation, and open my eyes to see how I can help strangers in need.

NELL GODDARD

Eternal hospitality

Then the angel said to me, 'Write this: Blessed are those who are invited to the wedding supper of the Lamb!' And he added, 'These are the true words of God.' (NIV)

What's the best party you've ever been to? Aged five, I went to a wedding reception. I still remember the utter delight of discovering that not only was the bride wearing a beautiful tiara (which she let me touch!), but that there was a HUGE bouncy castle.

Weddings are often some of the best parties – with good food, a free bar and plenty of joy to go around. And yet here on earth, weddings – and marriage itself – are but a symbol of what's to come and of God's covenant love for his own bride, the church.

I don't know whether there will be a bouncy castle in heaven at the wedding supper of the Lamb, although I'm pretty hopeful there will be. But what I do know for certain is that there will be good food, plenty to drink and a joy that overflows as the ultimate covenant is made between the bride and the bridegroom. Those who are invited are truly blessed.

In the book of Revelation, we see an image of God's ultimate hospitality. We are invited not just as guests but as the bride herself, beautifully dressed for her husband. Perhaps we, too, will wear a tiara.

Hospitality was God's idea in the first place – opening up his home, his life, his very self to those who were far off. And that invitation is still open. As the bride of Christ, it's our job to pass on the news, to share the invitation to those who might not have heard yet. So big is God's hospitality that there is room for all.

And this incredible hospitality will reach its ultimate conclusion at the wedding supper of the Lamb, and, bouncy castle or not, it truly will be the best party we've ever been to.

Father, thank you that we are invited to the wedding supper of the Lamb. Please give us the words and the courage to share the good news of the open invitation to the best party the world has ever seen.

NELL GODDARD

A doctor explores healing

Jennifer Rees Larcombe writes:

On 13 June 1990, I was healed suddenly after spending eight years dependent on a wheelchair. Because I was already quite well-known as a writer, my healing received a lot of media attention, so I was contacted by medical doctors who were interested to inspect my hospital records and interview my GP. One of these was Dr Jenny Davey. She had recently been healed herself from breast cancer and was beginning to see remarkable things happening as she prayed for her patients. She had been amazed to discover that God sometimes does things which she, with her years of training and experience, would find impossible. Ever since, she has been telling people what God did for her – and praying for them, too – because when you experience miraculous healing yourself, you know without a doubt that God still intervenes in human lives today.

During the next two weeks, we are going to looking at some healing accounts collected by another doctor. Luke was obviously as fascinated by the miraculous as Dr Jenny, having watched Paul praying for the sick in Greece during Paul's first missionary journey. He soon became a faithful member of Paul's travelling ministry team and was known as the 'beloved physician' (Colossians 4:14, KJV)

Luke never met Jesus himself, but he obviously loved listening to the stories of eyewitnesses who had: he probably met them during the two years Paul was imprisoned at Caesarea, not far from Jerusalem. I suspect that many of these stories were told to him by women, whose memories would not have been thought worthy of recounting by the Jewish men who wrote the other three gospels. At that time, Jewish culture would have discounted the testimony of women, but Luke, a Gentile, obviously honoured women and mentions them many more times than the other gospel writers. His beautifully detailed account of the birth of Jesus must surely have come from Mary herself.

Many scholars think that Theophilus (Luke 1:3), for whom Luke wrote his gospel and Acts, was a high-ranking Roman legal official amassing evidence for Paul's trial before the emperor. The testimony of a man of science like Luke would have been useful in authenticating the supernatural work of the Holy Spirit, which was the very essence of Paul's ministry.

Disappointed hope

There was a priest named Zechariah… His wife Elizabeth was also a descendant of Aaron. Both of them were righteous in the sight of God… But they were childless because Elizabeth was not able to conceive, and they were both very old. (NIV)

Why, when Luke was writing Jesus' biography, did he start with the story of someone else's birth? One reason may be that, as a doctor, he was so fascinated by God's ability to heal that he simply could not resist including it. During his career in medicine, he may often have experienced the frustration of not being able to help women who came to him because they could not conceive a baby. Without our modern technology, there was little he could do. So Elizabeth's case amazed him. Not only was she *steiros* (the gynecological term Luke used to describe her sterility), she was also far too old to conceive – yet she had borne a healthy son.

It was a huge honour to be picked to go through the curtains into the Holiest Place, but what should have been the greatest day in Zechariah's life was tinged with sadness because of the 'Why, Lord?' in his heart.

It is desperately hard to pray for many years for something, only to be endlessly disappointed. In those days, childlessness was a disgrace because, like any disability, it was seen as God's punishment for wickedness. Yet they had both lived godly lives – so why had God ignored their prayers?

It can be so easy to do and say all the right 'Christian' things outwardly, but inside disappointment can secretly turn our hearts cold towards the God who fails to give us that one thing we want most. Perhaps it was lost hope that made it hard for Zechariah to believe Gabriel's amazing message. Disillusionment with God makes discounting anything supernatural more comfortable than facing our hidden resentment.

Enjoy the picture of a dignified priest trying to describe an angel to a shocked crowd, using only hand signals!

Please show me, Lord, if hidden resentment is stunting the growth of my faith in your power.

JENNIFER REES LARCOMBE

A masterclass

Jesus left the synagogue and went to the home of Simon. Now Simon's mother-in-law was suffering from a high fever, and they asked Jesus to help her. So he bent over her and rebuked the fever, and it left her. She got up at once and began to wait on them. (NIV)

I sense Luke's excitement as he describes the day which launches Jesus' healing ministry. To set the scene: Jesus is emerging as a popular itinerant preacher, but recently he has had to escape from his home town, Nazareth, after infuriating neighbours by applying to himself a passage describing the Messiah. Avoiding the lynch mob, he has just arrived to make his home base by Lake Galilee in Capernaum. He startles the synagogue with a dramatic deliverance, and arrives at Peter's house to find the family in turmoil. Luke uses the medical term *suecho* to explain that Peter's mother-in-law is seriously ill with a virulent infection and running a dangerously high temperature.

Luke would have treated her using lengthy, elaborate medical procedures, so he is fascinated that Jesus merely leaned over her and said a few firm words. As the creator of the universe, Jesus realised harmful bacteria were attacking her blood cells, so he banished them, rather as modern antibiotics would do!

Luke is even more astonished by the speed of her recovery. He would expect that someone recovering from serious infection would need days of careful nursing and rest to regain their strength. But this woman got straight up and served lunch for a large group of people. I can believe that because, a few days after my own healing, I was examined by a physio who had known me throughout the eight years of my disability. She said, 'It should have taken months to get your muscles to this level of fitness.'

After what happened that evening in Capernaum, the town was constantly surging with crowds demanding healing. How do you think the locals felt about their new neighbour?

Lord, help me remember to recharge my batteries by spending time with you, as Jesus did. Please forgive me for so often thinking other things are more important.

JENNIFER REES LARCOMBE

What paralyses you?

'Which is easier: to say, "Your sins are forgiven," or to say, "Get up and walk"? But I want you to know that the Son of Man has authority on earth to forgive sins.' (NIV)

Far from being a sleepy fishing village, Capernaum was a thriving centre in a heavily populated region. Manufacturing industries and a Roman military camp provided employment, and the highway between Damascus and Jerusalem ran by, bringing customers for hoteliers and market traders. Business boomed still more when Jesus came home from one of his lengthy tours, and vast crowds of miracle-seekers filled the town. Luke is the only one who emphasises what a special day this was for the town. Eminent Pharisees, ultra-holy Bible teachers, came from everywhere to examine Jesus' doctrine. Was it the events of that day which formed their bad opinion of him – turning them into his enemies?

Their examination was going well until it was interrupted by a disturbance. Imagine the sticks and mud from the roof crashing on to those prestigious visitors! Worse still, Pharisees considered the stretcher-case as unclean, because of the incontinence connected with paralysis. They would have pulled their robes away in disgust. By contrast, Jesus uses a particularly intimate name to address the man. It is translated 'Friend', but means something more like 'my own beloved child or soul mate'.

We are hugely influenced by what other people think of us, but it's only Jesus' opinion that counts. Everyone expected to see a healing miracle, but, like any good doctor, Luke knew spiritual healing is as important as physical. The man's greatest need was forgiveness – Jesus knew he was tortured by guilt, perhaps after something he did before being disabled. Fortunately, unlike others, Jesus never judges us by outward appearances. The Pharisees were infuriated, and even more so when Jesus claimed to be the Messiah by calling himself 'the Son of Man' (see Daniel 7:13).

When we've been ill a long time, our faith for healing can dwindle – mine did. That's why we badly need faithful praying friends.

We can be paralysed by fear, shame or unforgiveness. Ask the Lord if there is anything that is preventing you from becoming the woman Jesus designed you to be. If you sense his 'yes', then explore healing prayer.

JENNIFER REES LARCOMBE

Doing the unthinkable

Jesus reached out his hand and touched the man. 'I am willing,' he said. 'Be clean!' And immediately the leprosy left him. (NIV)

A leper dashed from the hills as Jesus was walking by and waylaid him. It was totally illegal for him to come so close to civilisation or to speak to anyone. Can we stop a moment to imagine this man's distress? When the first white leprosy spots appeared, he was forced to leave his wife and children homeless – because their house had to be demolished and all possessions destroyed. Driven out to camp alone in the wild, he had lost everything: his job, parents, friends, synagogue and community. Someone might bring him food but never came close enough to speak. I often wonder if the thing he missed most was human touch: a hug, supportive handshakes, even a smile or kind remark – all he got were angry shouts and painful stones.

Maybe friends left notes describing the amazing healer, so he longed to meet Jesus. But leprosy was seen as a punishment for sin, so would this holy man want to help? Jesus' action was unnecessary as well as illegal – Luke describes others he healed from a distance (Luke 7:10). Yet Jesus reached out towards that revolting figure no one had been near for years, and the touch of his hand healed the man's lonely, despairing soul as well as his diseased body.

What did Jesus tell the man *not* to do? The growing crowds who flocked after Jesus were becoming a dangerous problem. They wanted a Messiah to drive out the Romans, so rebels plotted to make Jesus king by force (John 6:15), but Jesus did not want war and death – he came to bring life and peace!

Thank you, Lord, that you don't only notice successful people; you also love outcasts, the lonely and rejected, failures and misfits too. You never treat us as others do – please help us to do the same.

JENNIFER REES LARCOMBE

Enemy spies

A man was there whose right hand was shrivelled. The Pharisees and the teachers of the law were looking for a reason to accuse Jesus, so they watched him closely to see if he would heal on the Sabbath. (NIV)

The front rows of the synagogue (the seats reserved for VIPs) were filled with a delegation of Pharisees, dispatched from the Sanhedrin, whose role was to punish anyone who misled the public. It had been like this ever since the 'man through the roof' incident: Jesus had been constantly spied on and attacked, not by evil men but by ultra-religious people who had forgotten that God's commandments are about loving God and bringing love and peace to others. They even forced everyone to keep extra commandments they had created themselves. Luke tells us what Jesus thought about them (11:42, 46).

Squashed at the back of the synagogue with other paupers was a man with a useless right hand: the word Luke uses reveals the man lost its use after an injury. Apocryphal accounts (stories about Jesus not included in the Bible) say that this man had been a highly respected, prosperous stonemason, now unemployed, homeless and reduced to begging to feed his children.

Technically, Jesus did not even break their sabbath laws; the man didn't ask for healing and Jesus never touched him or rubbed him with anything (John 9:6). But still they obstinately objected. Jesus could see the joy it would bring to this man's whole family if he was healed, but his enemies only cared about their petty rules.

Their cold hearts and critical attitudes hurt and enraged Jesus (Mark 3:5); they were breaking his heart. We Christians do the same to Jesus when we criticise each other or fall out over unimportant details.

Luke tells us for the third time how Jesus went off to be alone with his Father. That is also the best thing for us to do when we are hurt and upset.

Do you have an unused skill – such as worship-leading, baking, singing, art or writing? Like this man's right hand, might Jesus want you to 'stretch out' this area of your life towards him so that he can restore and use it again?

JENNIFER REES LARCOMBE

21

An intriguing story

'I did not even consider myself worthy to come to you. But say the word, and my servant will be healed.' (NIV)

As an itinerant speaker myself for 28 years, I can imagine Jesus arriving home after a tour with a sigh of relief. But even here he faced constant demands (Mark 6:31). I wonder if these local synagogue elders included Jairus (8:41)? It obviously suited them to bend their usually rigid rules on this occasion – why? Roman slaves were normally kicked out to die when they were too ill or old to be useful – they had no rights. Notice how unusually this one was treated. In war films, enemy officers are usually depicted as brutally cruel, and most Romans despised Jews. Was it this man's belief in God which made him so different?

Luke always speaks kindly of centurions in both Acts and his gospel, perhaps because he was writing to a high-ranking Roman official on Paul's behalf (1:3). The man's enormous faith in Jesus' ability to heal intrigues me most of all in this story. Maybe he was friends with another Capernaum resident, a nobleman whose son Jesus healed from a distance (John 4:46–52)? He also understood chains of command: when Caesar gave a command in Rome, an event was soon activated thousands of miles away simply because everyone obeyed orders. Astonishingly, he addressed Jesus as Lord – *Kuros* – a title Romans reserved for Caesar alone.

Do we have to deserve our healing? When I was ill, Christians were constantly telling me what I was doing, or not doing, that prevented my healing. After eight years, I'd tried everything they suggested. Then I realised, at last, that we can never, ever, earn healing by good behaviour. It's a mysterious gift of grace.

Lord, I often feel unworthy to speak to you. Help me to remember that you are always willing to communicate, regardless of our race, creed or experience in prayer. All you need is our wordless look of faith.

JENNIFER REES LARCOMBE

Tragedy transformed

As he approached the town gate, a dead person was being carried out – the only son of his mother, and she was a widow… When the Lord saw her, his heart went out to her. (NIV)

The huge crowd of 'Jesus-groupies' must have felt tired after following him, on foot, 25 miles from Capernaum in blistering heat. As they climbed the steep hill to the large town of Nain, were they thinking about the drink and supper they'd enjoy once they arrived? Frustration! They were held up by another large throng – a funeral procession led by flutes, cymbals and professional wailers.

Luke, the only one who tells this story, must have heard it from someone who was there and who noticed that Jesus wasn't annoyed, even if his followers were. He saw the solitary woman, bowed with grief, walking in front of a wickerwork stretcher. He knew that without her son she would be destitute and utterly alone. Luke uses the Greek word which describes the deepest possible compassion to describe Jesus' expression. The sudden atmosphere shift when the corpse sat up would have been indescribably dramatic!

Everyone knew that raising the dead would be a major proof of the Messiah's identity, so to do that before so many witnesses was probably very dangerous, particularly when massive public interest in Jesus was becoming such a major political concern. However, to Jesus, one obscure, poverty-stricken widow was worth any risk.

This story, happy though it is, may cause pain. If you have lost someone you love, in spite of much earnest prayer, you may have been left with the agonising question: 'Why does Jesus heal some and not others?' There are no answers this side of heaven – healing is God's private mystery. A six-year-old explained it like this: 'God's bigger than us, and cleverer, so we just have to let him sort it.'

Lord, help me to remember that knowing you does not bring immunity from sorrow but ensures your love and comfort in sorrow.

JENNIFER REES LARCOMBE

Complete healing

As Jesus was climbing out of the boat, a man who was possessed by demons came out to meet him... As soon as he saw Jesus, he... screamed, 'Why are you interfering with me, Jesus, Son of the Most High God?' (NLT)

Poor disciples! When, after the storm, they finally landed, in the dark, on a deserted beach surrounded by graves, eerie screams traumatised them further as a naked man hurtled towards them. Why was he there? Was he demonised or mentally ill? I believe he was both. Perhaps, during Roman occupation, he had witnessed some frightful atrocity from which he had never recovered. The demonic is attracted by emotional wounds, so evil spirits invaded and were using his derangement to spread fear throughout the area. Supernatural strength helped him break his chains, escape his guards to wander the hills at night, shrieking and self-harming (Mark 5:5). He obviously felt he had an entire regiment of devils tormenting him. What convinces me that he was more than just mentally ill was his instant recognition of who Jesus actually was. Even the disciples had not yet reached that point.

Why did Jesus not just send the demons direct to the pit to await judgement, rather than involving the pigs? He didn't usually work that way. Maybe the local people would not have been convinced the man was finally healed without tangible proof.

Fear seems to dominate this whole occasion. The disciples had been afraid of drowning and panicked by the power Jesus had over the storm. The demons were petrified of Jesus, the pigs were terrified, the farmers were scared and soon the whole district was so frightened of the supernatural that they ordered Jesus to leave. In the middle of so much terror, one beautifully peaceful scene stands out: the once-wild man, washed, dressed and sitting close to Jesus as they all enjoyed breakfast round a driftwood fire. Dr Luke is delighted to describe the man as *sozo*, meaning restored in body, mind and spirit -- completely whole.

Mark 5:20 tells us what a successful evangelist this man became, but it can be difficult to talk to our family and friends about our faith. We all need to pray, 'Lord, give me the right words at the right time.'

JENNIFER REES LARCOMBE

The frantic father

Then Jesus took her by the hand and said in a loud voice, 'My child, get up!' And at that moment her life returned, and she immediately stood up! Then Jesus told them to give her something to eat. (NLT)

As Jesus stepped on to Capernaum's quay, the usual demanding crowds surged to meet him; but most unusually, they parted deferentially to make way for the most respected member of the community, Jairus. How hard it would have been for the prosperous administrative head of the synagogue to enlist the help of the renegade rabbi who was turning the area upside down and threatening the status quo!

Even more astounding is that he knelt before Jesus so publicly. No Jew ever knelt to anyone but God or his anointed king (Esther 3:2). Was Jairus beginning to suspect Jesus was who he said he was – perhaps through the influence of his friend, the Roman centurion?

With time running out for his girl, Jairus was frantic when – to him – an utterly unimportant woman delayed Jesus. Then suddenly it was all too late. Have you ever felt like giving up on Jesus when he didn't seem able, or interested enough, to do what you badly needed him to do? Did you then feel he was asking you to trust him just a little bit longer? I have. Perhaps Jairus was too numb to respond.

At the point of death, loud wailing would spread the news and the house would be filled with weeping neighbours. Verse 52 has caused sceptics to think the girl was merely in a coma, but Jesus said the same of Lazarus when he had been dead for four days (John 11:11–13). Obviously, Jesus knew their 'deaths' were only temporary. Perhaps Jesus put the sceptical mourners out so firmly because he wanted to keep this story as quiet as possible.

How tender of Jesus to break all laws and taboos by touching death yet again and by waking the girl so gently. I can't recall rousing my teenagers as affectionately!

Lord, I sometimes feel angry with you when you allow tragedy to hit good people's lives. Please forgive me; underneath I recognise that bad times definitely offer the chance to move closer to you for your help and comfort.
                                                    JENNIFER REES LARCOMBE

How Jesus sees us

'Who touched me?' Jesus asked… Peter said, 'Master, the people are crowding and pressing against you.' But Jesus said, 'Someone touched me; I know that power has gone out from me.' (NIV)

Many of the stories Luke selected feature underdogs, and he mentions women more often than the other gospel writers. Today's heroine was both. Her embarrassing condition made her unclean and separated her from contact with people, including her husband and children. Mark 5:26 says she was destitute; all her money was spent on doctors who put her through painful, humiliating cures which failed to help. (Luke, loyal to fellow medics, leaves that bit out!)

To have developed such a high level of faith, she must have heard and watched Jesus from a distance but dared not approach him and had no one to ask him on her behalf. Perhaps her only chance came when everyone's attention was focused on Jairus and his crisis. Unnoticed, she slid among the jostling crowd and reached out a trembling hand.

Suddenly, everything stopped! The crowd fell back; she was alone and exposed. Jairus, the most important person in town, looked down at the least important. Was he enraged at her interruption? Jesus also looked down, but with eyes full of understanding and love.

It would be impossible for her to know instantly that her bleeding had stopped, but she knew she was healed – by faith! It was the same for me. I simply stepped out of my wheelchair in front of the amazed congregation.

She would never have forgotten that moment with Jesus. After years of being ignored and rejected, he made her feel valued and important by tenderly calling her 'daughter' – a beautifully intimate name.

There is usually a 'problem' person in every church. They lurch from one crisis to the next and, however much prayer they receive, never seem to get well. Most of us try to avoid them – unless we want to follow Jesus' example!

Thank you, Lord Jesus, that you love each one of us as if we were the only one to love. You are never in a rush and never too busy to give us your full attention.

JENNIFER REES LARCOMBE

Do it now!

Jesus asked, 'Were not all ten cleansed? Where are the other nine? Has no one returned to give praise to God except this foreigner?' (NIV)

Yet again, Luke highlights a Gentile. Remember he was writing for Gentile readers in Rome. He wanted to emphasise that Jesus came to rescue Jews and Gentiles alike (John 3:16).

Jesus was on his last journey to Jerusalem, knowing he would die there.

Unlike the previous leper Luke described, these men did not approach Jesus but shouted from the legal distance of 50 yards. This time, Jesus did not touch them; he merely shouted instructions. Luke would have spent years learning the 'right and only' method to treat every ailment, so he was obviously fascinated that Jesus healed every sick person differently. Can you think of some of the other ways Jesus used for healing people?

Because a particular prayer method seems to bring healing to one person, people write books and build ministries based on it. We get upset and feel like failures when it 'doesn't work' for us, but Jesus treats each of us as a unique VIP.

I can identify with their joy as the lepers suddenly realised they were cured, during their sprint to find the nearest priest! The morning after my sudden healing, I woke at five and went for a glorious walk in the park – no wheelchair, no carer – just me and God. I felt intoxicated with joy as I sang praise songs! I am sure all ten felt like that, too, but only one returned to make a relationship with Jesus – which would have led on to even more blessing. The others probably meant to thank him – one day – but never had another chance.

Have you ever felt God was asking you to do something, but you put it off until 'life gets easier', and somehow it never happened? The tenth man knew the benefit of the 'do it now' rule!

Lord, I am very sorry that I so often ask you for things, then completely forget to say thank you! That must hurt you so badly; and it hurts me too, because being grumbly and discontented makes me feel terrible!

JENNIFER REES LARCOMBE

Healing an enemy

When Jesus' followers saw what was going to happen... one of them struck the servant of the high priest, cutting off his right ear. But Jesus answered, 'No more of this!' And he touched the man's ear and healed him. (NIV)

Luke, with a doctor's fascination, gives us three healings not mentioned by the other gospel writers: the woman bent double by severe scoliosis (13:10–14); the man with heart failure or 'abnormal swelling' (14:1–4); and today's story, which I believe is the most beautiful of them all.

The men who came to arrest Jesus represented his worst enemies. Throughout his ministry they had spied on, criticised, persecuted and accused him. That Jesus should heal one of them is amazing – in a situation like that, most of us would feel like cutting off the other ear to match! Back in Luke 6:27 Jesus had said, 'Love your enemies, do good to those who hate you.' Now, at the worst time of his life, he is practising what he preached. Could Jesus be asking you to do something kind for the person who hurt you so badly? I have found doing that has often made forgiving easier.

As Judas stepped out of the shadows, Peter must have been shocked to realise why he had left supper so early. The disciples were massively outnumbered by well-armed men (only having two swords between them). John tells us it was Peter who, typically failing to wait for permission, lunged at the man who was probably the leader. His action could have triggered terrible bloodshed – the last thing Jesus wanted was to see his beloved friends wounded and dying around him. He needed them to escape quickly and quietly so they could take his message to the world. His curt command saved them all. John 18:10 also tells us that the injured man was called Malchus, servant of the high priest. I wonder if, like Bartimaeus, the fact that we know his name means he later became a well-known follower of Jesus.

Perhaps, like the hymn writer Isaac Watts, Malchus thought, 'Were the whole realm of nature mine, that were an offering far too small, love so amazing, so divine demands my soul, my life, my all.'

JENNIFER REES LARCOMBE

Jesus the teacher:
Mark 1—10

Tracy Williamson writes:

When I was asked to write these notes on the theme of 'Jesus the teacher', my initial reaction was 'Help!' I am not theologically trained and knew that I wouldn't be able to glean lots of interesting detail and background information from the passages. Was I the best person to do it?

Well, I probably wasn't the 'best' person, but as I prayed God put a 'yes' in my heart and I knew that it was right for me to do this series. I have found it a very soul-searching group of passages, and I hope that comes over in the way I've written the notes. The scriptures took me from Jesus' great love for his Father and desire to listen to his Father's voice and do his works, to his grief when God gets pushed aside because we've become fixated on our own greatness or ways of doing things.

Writing these notes for others has taken me on my own journey of discovery to meet with Jesus in guises that are different to how I usually see him. As well as Jesus my Lord, saviour and friend, I've met the Jesus of holy anger; the Jesus of great understanding; the Jesus of tender love; Jesus the Son; Jesus who is strong in his ability to confront sin; and Jesus who never stops loving us and never gives up on us.

It is an awesome privilege to know Jesus and begin, through these verses, to understand in a deeper way what matters to him.

I found a longing growing within me as I wrote, to 'shake off everything that hinders' and press on in my walk with God. I would so love to live my life as a true expression of his amazing love, and I want to give him permission to work within my heart to heal and release me from all negativity. It is God's joy, through the Holy Spirit, to help us become more and more like Jesus – so if that is your prayer too, I know he will bless it.

My thoughts and commentary are only one person's exploration of what God might be saying through each day's passage. I hope and pray they will bless and inspire you, but most of all that you will go deeper in your own reading and on an exciting journey into God's heart.

A teacher with authority

The people were all so amazed that they asked each other, 'What is this? A new teaching – and with authority! He even gives orders to impure spirits and they obey him.' News about him spread quickly over the whole region of Galilee. (NIV)

Recently, someone's endorsement of my new book really thrilled me. He said, 'Tracy writes with the gentle authority of the Holy Spirit.' Wow! Demonstrating God's authority is one of those awesome hallmarks of being a Christian and having the presence of Jesus living within us.

If the authority of Jesus can be seen in us, what exactly is it? What amazed the local people so much that they exclaimed over his authority? There was something different and compelling that they could both see and hear in Jesus. What was different was where the teaching came from. The Pharisees and teachers of the law taught rules that they'd twisted to increase their own power. They bullied and judged, but Jesus had a true authority of gentleness and peace, combined with the certainty born of heart-knowledge of God's supremacy.

Did Jesus shout to show his authority? I doubt it, though he must have 'upped' the volume simply to reach the listening crowds of people! What gripped their attention, however, was Jesus' personal knowledge of God. Jesus revealed God as Father in a way no one else could. His words came from a heart that was saturated with his Father's ways and character. When Jesus was confronted by the evil spirit, he simply said, 'Be quiet! Come out of him!' and the spirit obeyed.

Knowing our right and power through Jesus to stand against Satan is an awesome calling that we all share. We too can reveal that quiet, sure authority that Jesus exhibited. A minister once spent two hours shouting at the devil to leave someone receiving ministry. Another leader arrived and in a quiet, firm voice declared that the person belonged to Jesus. And that was it; the battle was over – God's awesome authority in action today, through a believer who knew Jesus.

We only truly come to know someone by spending quality time with them. Read Exodus 34:6–8. Just as God revealed his character to Moses, ask him to give you a new revelation of what he is like.

TRACY WILLIAMSON

Spending time with the Father

Very early in the morning, while it was still dark, Jesus got up, left the house and went off to a solitary place, where he prayed. (NIV)

I love learning about Jesus' spiritual life. His authority rested on his knowing God as Father, and it seems he created time and space to make that knowing possible. He needed to be with his Father, to hear his voice and to see what he was doing. In John 5:19, he said that he could do nothing but what he saw his Father doing. Like a small child learning from watching its parents, so Jesus needed to listen to God and see his heart through the revelation of the Holy Spirit.

If Jesus needed to listen to God, how much more do we? We can't just rely on what we heard in the sermon a week ago; we need a daily encounter with God. Jesus made that choice, organising his day so that he could meet with his Father whatever pressures he was facing. Their relationship was a partnership, as ours must be too.

Do we view spending time with God as an obligation or as something desirable and exciting, like spending time with a favourite friend? What can motivate us? The key is the realisation that God longs to encounter and bless us during our time with him. When Jesus was baptised, God spoke audibly from heaven, saying that he was 'well pleased' with his Son. God delights in affirming his children and giving us wisdom to know how to live our lives. When the disciples found Jesus after his prayer time and told him off for vanishing, he responded with a plan to 'go to the nearby villages and preach', because 'that is why I have come'. His times with God empowered him to know his mission and empowered him with God's love and compassion. How does God want to bless and empower you?

Think about your everyday commitments. Is there a particular time that you can consider as God's? Can you assign a special chair or room as your 'meeting place'? Ask him how he wants to bless and guide you today.

TRACY WILLIAMSON

Knowing his goal

On hearing this, Jesus said to them, 'It is not the healthy who need a doctor, but those who are ill. I have not come to call the righteous, but sinners.' (NIV)

Have you ever heard a sermon that's packed so full of impressive words and concepts you're left wondering what's being taught? Maybe it's just me, but I leave such services feeling deflated. God seems too far off for me to reach or understand.

The teachers of the law and Pharisees loved teaching in this way, but Jesus was different. His words reflected the way he lived and he lived out the truth of his words. He loved and understood the ordinary people and taught, prayed and acted in such a way that they were constantly thrilled, inspired and made hungry to know more. Verse 2 says, 'They gathered in such large numbers that there was no room left, not even outside the door, and he preached the word to them.' What was drawing them to listen so intently and in such numbers? What comes over to me is how focused his teaching was. In modern jargon, he knew his 'market' and he had a goal: to call sinners to God.

When we know who we are aiming to reach and what our goal is, our teaching has a powerful new dimension. Jesus wasn't speaking to show how knowledgeable he was, but to touch ordinary people and draw them into God's love. His declaration of forgiveness over the paralysed man was a dynamic expression of God's grace; his calling of Levi and his enjoying a meal at Levi's home with his tax-collector friends were visibly teaching God's heart of friendship. It's no wonder that the teachers of the law were offended, as he was threatening their whole way of being. Jesus demonstrated that when words and actions are rooted in the power of God's love, then God's holy authority is activated. The paralysed man walked, sinners' lives were transformed and crowds drew close to God.

God created you with unique gifts to show people what he is like. Tell him you want to be rooted in the power of his love and anointed with his authority.

TRACY WILLIAMSON

New wine, old wineskins

'No one pours new wine into old wineskins. Otherwise, the wine will burst the skins, and both the wine and the wineskins will be ruined. No, they pour new wine into new wineskins.' (NIV)

Today, I am struck by how 'real' Jesus' teaching was. He loved stories from everyday life, vivid illustrations that made people think about their lives and faith in a new way. He rooted concepts that were life-changing in the language of everyday experiences that all could identify with. This is the wonder of partnership with the Holy Spirit. He takes ordinary things and opens our eyes to deep spiritual truths hidden within them.

Everyone understood processes like patching holes in clothes or making wine, but Jesus wanted them to think, to join the dots together and to experience the wonder of understanding a deeper truth. The old wineskins represented the rigid mindset of their traditional beliefs and rules.

This discussion was in the context of Jesus eating with Levi and his friends, which offended many because it went against their fixed view that tax collectors were only fit to be condemned. They expressed their displeasure by focusing on other things that seemed obviously wrong, such as Jesus' disciples not fasting. Jesus' reply was very telling: 'How can the guests of the bridegroom fast while he is with them?' If they'd just listened and understood, they could have known such joy and wonder, but their minds were fixed in a certain way and, like those old wineskins, couldn't hold anything new. The bridegroom, the long-awaited Messiah, was with them, but they were blind to him because of their fixation on rules and rituals.

Jesus wasn't dismissing fasting – when done with the right motives, it is a key to effective prayer and intimacy with God. However, at that moment they had the greatest opportunity ever to be intimate with God and discover the power of prayer. Sadly, they were old wineskins and couldn't accommodate the power of the new. Do I do any better?

Lord, I know that sometimes I just don't want to be open to a new perspective. Please forgive and change me so I can receive the wonder and joy of all you want to show me of your love and power.

TRACY WILLIAMSON

Teaching from his heart

Jesus asked them, 'Which is lawful on the Sabbath: to do good or to do evil, to save life or to kill?' But they remained silent. He looked around at them in anger and, deeply distressed at their stubborn hearts, said to the man, 'Stretch out your hand.' (NIV)

Sometimes Bible teachers can seem lacking in passion, but Jesus was very different. His heart was rooted in the Father's love and from that base he burned with a passion for people to respond to what he was teaching them about God. He was often described as 'moved with compassion' for those in deep need, but on this occasion he was angry and distressed. Those he loved were also causing him anger. It is a sobering thought, especially knowing that he had no sin. He wasn't like us, who lash out in anger just because we've had a bad day; he was angry for a reason – their stubbornness of heart.

We think of stubbornness as a character trait, the mark of someone who sticks their heels in. But in this case the stubbornness ran deeper. Jesus was distressed because of their condemning and destructive attitudes. They were in the synagogue. It should have been a time for worshipping God, but instead they were looking for a way to bring him down. A sick man was among them, with the opportunity for Jesus to lovingly meet his need, but they didn't care about the man. All they cared about was seeing if Jesus broke their rules. So from his heart of pain, he taught them the true meaning of the sabbath: to know God, to save life, to do good. And then he fulfilled his teaching by healing the man. The Pharisees' response? Plotting together 'how they might kill Jesus'.

It's easy for us to judge the Pharisees, but do we need to look at our own heart responses too? Am I causing Jesus distress by my rigid or judgemental attitudes? How does Jesus want to change me so that my life reflects God's heart of compassion?

Father, I am sorry for all my stubbornness and wrong attitudes. Please give me the humility to admit my need of change. Melt my heart with your love. Please help me never to cause you pain or anger.

TRACY WILLIAMSON

Confronting false accusation

And the teachers of the law who came down from Jerusalem said, 'He is possessed by Beelzebul! By the prince of demons he is driving out demons.' (NIV)

When I am judged, I feel crushed, agonising over everything and sometimes reacting defensively and blaming others in my turn. How can we react to accusation in a godly way?

Here, we see Jesus bombarded by accusations about his identity. Even his family came to take charge of him, declaring that he was out of his mind. The teachers of the law proclaimed the most terrible of judgements, that it was by the prince of demons that Jesus was casting out demons.

Why did people make such destructive, false accusations? I believe it was their fear. Some of Jesus' miracles were prophesied in Isaiah as the work of the Messiah: miracles that only the Messiah would be able to do. The Pharisees were terrified that they would have to admit he was the Messiah, so they lashed out, saying in effect that Jesus was a murderer and idolater.

I find Jesus' response deeply challenging. His words were full of godly reasoning, focusing on the impossibility of Satan being able to successfully cast out demons without destroying himself. Jesus didn't lash out, mock or retaliate. But he did warn them, in a very calm but gravely serious way, of the eternal repercussions should they continue labelling the work of the Spirit 'satanic': 'Whoever blasphemes against the Holy Spirit will never be forgiven; they are guilty of an eternal sin'.

Jesus responded in grace and truth. He knew scripture. He understood those who were against him and was not overwhelmed by their lies, because he rested in God. In conclusion, he declared that those who do God's will are his true family.

Will I choose to be family to him in all my words, deeds and thoughts?

Are you distressed right now because you have been falsely accused? I believe God is saying to you, 'Don't be afraid, my child. Relax, for I am with you and will uphold you. I love you with an everlasting love.'

TRACY WILLIAMSON

Listen

'Whoever has ears to hear, let them hear.' (NIV)

Here, we see Jesus excelling in his gift as storyteller teacher, using parables – those little stories from everyday life with a powerful message that he expects his listeners to unravel for themselves.

Jesus prefaced his teaching with the directive, 'Listen.' He wanted them to truly hear and understand what he was telling them. I find that meaningful because, as a deaf person, I have to make a conscious effort to ensure that I understand. I can't chat casually with someone in the kitchen because their words just wash over me. I have to deliberately listen and pay attention. Even then, I will only be able to follow so much and will often ask the person to sit with me and type on my iPad to be certain I've understood.

Jesus commands the crowds to listen in a focused way as he tells the story of the farmer sowing his seed. He wants them to engage with the story and personalise it, finding its true meaning as they reflect. All of the seeds are destined to grow and bear fruit, but only one lot of these seeds will do so, those that land on the good soil. The rocks, thistles, pathways and birds will destroy the rest.

As with all of Jesus' teaching, there is personal challenge: will I take time to perceive and understand his word to me? Will I seek to ensure I grow in my life and in my relationship to God, or will I just react as a victim when bad things happen? Will I take time to search out what the hard ground, rocks and thorns represent in my life, and with God's help get rid of them? What constitutes the 'good soil' for his words to take root in my life and bear their fruit?

Lord Jesus, thank you for constantly sowing your powerful words in my life. Help me to change those areas within me that choke your seeds of truth. I long to listen and to grow.

TRACY WILLIAMSON

The kingdom of heaven

'[The kingdom of heaven] is like a mustard seed, which is the smallest of all seeds on earth. Yet when planted, it grows and becomes the largest of all garden plants, with such big branches that the birds can perch in its shade.' (NIV)

Are you hungry to know what heaven is like and to see God's glory here on earth? I am. In these parables, Jesus taps into our inner longing to be with the Father and see his kingdom. Jesus wants us to understand its beauty and power, so he feeds us with these glimpses into heavenly realities. The effect is like when we see a film trailer and can't wait to see the whole film. Their underlying message in Jesus' parables of supernatural growth inspires our faith and challenges our cultural mindset, that we need to be powerful and successful in ourselves. In the farming parable of verses 26–29, the man scatters the seed and, without any striving on his part, it grows. Jesus says the soil produces corn all by itself.

This was and is a powerful word. In the guise of faith, we can follow the god of self-made perfection, with our cultural emphasis on making ourselves, realising our dreams and excelling.

Jesus was showing a different reality and a far more dynamic one. We must not be embarrassed by our smallness, for God uses the weak and small, filling them with his power so they grow and spread. What starts off tiny like the mustard seed grows into the largest possible bush, even sheltering birds that don't habitually nest in such bushes. That is a prophetic picture of how through God's kingdom, everyone will be reached. One seed is destined to become a harvest. How exciting and how important to realise that, however small we feel ourselves to be, we too are destined to show his glory as we grow and nurture others.

God wants to encourage you in all you are doing to serve him. He is saying, 'Never dismiss your work for me as being insignificant. It is creating amazing and beautiful fruit because you are serving in my love.'

TRACY WILLIAMSON

Closed hearts

'Where did this man get these things?' they asked. 'What's this wisdom that has been given him? What are these remarkable miracles he is performing? Isn't this the carpenter? Isn't this Mary's son and the brother of James, Joseph, Judas and Simon?...' And they took offence at him. (NIV)

Have you ever felt that you no longer belong with those you grew up with? Maybe your own family have rejected you because you have changed, and you feel alone in the midst of those closest to you. Jesus understands. Rejection hurts and it affected Jesus deeply; it made it impossible for him to do many miracles among them. The sad thing is that those listening to him recognised that there was something different about his words. They knew it was wisdom; they were being given a glimpse into what it meant to know God and experience his power. But all they could think of was that Jesus had changed. It offended them because it shook their security. Jesus was the carpenter. He had probably made some of their furniture. His mother and siblings were still among them, so how could he be the Messiah?

Jesus was 'amazed at their lack of faith' and 'could not do any miracles there, except lay his hands on a few people who were ill and heal them'.

That makes me wonder what Jesus was planning to do, had their reactions been different. He knew the town personally; had he planned with his Father to do something incredible? I am only surmising, but the fact is that the community's hostility rendered him unable to do very much. It is challenging to realise how much our small-mindedness can hinder God's work.

If you are struggling with the pain of rejection, Jesus cares deeply. Rejection can be paralysing, but Jesus still prayed for insight about what to do next and carried on teaching in the nearby villages. With his power and grace, we too can know peace and move forward into all he has for us.

God says to you: beloved child, I am with you and have plans for you. Don't let the attitudes of those closest to you define you negatively. You are the apple of my eye and I know the plans I have for you.

TRACY WILLIAMSON

Teaching through signs and wonders

Taking the five loaves and the two fish and looking up to heaven, he gave thanks and broke the loaves. Then he gave them to his disciples to distribute to the people. He also divided the two fish among them all. (NIV)

What was Jesus teaching his disciples through the feeding of the 5,000? The situation arose out of their need to spend quality time with Jesus. They'd returned from preaching the good news and seeing God do amazing things. Now they needed to share their experiences with Jesus, but such a large crowd gathered that they couldn't even eat. Jesus took them off for some time alone, but when they arrived the crowd had gone before them. The disciples must have felt exasperated; I know I would have! Jesus' reaction was different. He felt compassion for the crowd, because he could see they were 'like sheep without a shepherd'. Jesus reveals God's patience and loving-kindness through his reaction to things that simply irritate most people.

Jesus could see the crowd's heart-hunger to know something greater than themselves. I think that deeper need, as much as their physical hunger, was what motivated him to give them a miraculous meal. He knew what they really needed. Jesus sees the needs that we do not see ourselves. As we listen to him, he reveals our real needs, so that we might become open to his Spirit. I was upset recently that I kept putting off important work. Jesus showed me that my childhood fear of being mocked was making me run away from responsibility. I was amazed as that had never occurred to me, and I'm now asking him to heal that area of need.

Jesus teaches that God is bigger than our circumstances, and his compassion is with us in our struggles. Only God could cause bread to multiply enough to feed that enormous crowd. When the disciples were still floundering in their superficial reactions, he gave them this amazing lesson in ministering God's resources so that they too might become channels of the miraculous.

Thank you, Lord, that you know me completely. Please work in my heart that I will have the boldness to step out and partner with you in doing your amazing works.

TRACY WILLIAMSON

Is your heart healthy?

'Don't you see that nothing that enters a person from the outside can defile them? For it doesn't go into their heart but into their stomach, and then out of the body.' (NIV)

How healthy is your heart? Jesus' teaching can turn us inside out and make us take a long hard look at why we act as we do. When the Pharisees asked Jesus why his disciples were not doing all the acts of ritual cleansing that they'd set in place, Jesus was scathing in his response, quoting Isaiah's words: 'These people honour me with their lips, but their hearts are far from me. They worship me in vain; their teachings are merely human rules.'

Jesus makes it clear that God is looking for love, kindness and faithfulness as the true evidence of our faith – not just ritualistic actions that might be hiding things like greed, malice or sexual immorality. It's easy to point the finger at the Pharisees, but what is going on in our own hearts beneath the outward show of our particular way of being a Christian or doing church? Impassioned worship or exercising spiritual gifts can mask thoughts and attitudes we'd prefer others not to know about.

When I first joined Marilyn Baker in her singing ministry, I started sharing pictures and prophecies in all her concerts. One day, when asking the Spirit for a prophecy he said, 'When are you going to forgive your stepfather?' I was shocked! I'd been trying to hide my negative feelings behind the 'glory' of giving prophecies; but it was only once I allowed God's love to start melting away my anger that those prophetic words became effective, because they were springing from a place of true thankfulness and joy.

Is it time to ask Jesus to strip away any mask you too may be hiding behind?

Lord, thank you for the power of your forgiveness and your amazing love. Forgive me for my bad attitudes. Please cleanse and heal me deep down, so that my life will be full of your love from the inside out.

TRACY WILLIAMSON

What are you eating?

The disciples had forgotten to bring bread, except for one loaf they had with them in the boat. 'Be careful' Jesus warned them. 'Watch out for the yeast of the Pharisees and that of Herod.' (NIV)

I feel for Jesus and the disciples in this misunderstanding. As a deaf person, I often only understand half a situation and get confused trying to join the dots together. A silly example – I was having tea with my mum and she pointed out some cold meat on the side. I thought she was saying I could have more, but I'd had enough so I put it away. Later, I discovered that she'd put the meat aside for Goldie, my dog, not for me!

In this instance, Jesus was saying that the disciples needed to be on their guard against the 'yeast of the Pharisees'. What did he mean? Was it that they had no bread? The disciples were confused, but as Jesus said, they'd just witnessed him miraculously feeding thousands on two occasions. He was the bread of life, the prophet who could turn the very stones into bread if he so chose. But despite those miracles, they didn't understand that Jesus wasn't talking about bread, but about the Pharisees' teaching and their many crippling rules.

How can we avoid spiritual misunderstandings and allow the things we experience of God to take deeper root?

There is a key verse about Mary in Luke 2:51: 'But his mother treasured all these things in her heart.' Treasuring and taking in God's truths are vital. There was so much going on around Jesus' birth that it would have been easy for Mary to feel overwhelmed, but she chose to treasure the important things – to reflect upon the prophetic words, to celebrate all that God was doing, to think about the various encounters.

How are we spiritually eating? Are we feasting on God's words of truth, chewing them over, studying and memorising them so that no lies or misunderstandings can hinder our spiritual growth?

Father, thank you that you love to communicate and fill my heart with good news. Please open my heart to receive all you have for me. Help me to treasure you and so to grow.

TRACY WILLIAMSON

The heart of it

He took a little child whom he placed among them. Taking the child in his arms, he said to them, 'Whoever welcomes one of these little children in my name welcomes me.' (NIV)

Do you ever feel overwhelmed? In this passage, the disciples are flailing around in a fog of confusion as Jesus teaches them. Their hopes of a rich time together are shattered when he refers to the Son of Man being betrayed, killed and then rising again. This is such terrible news that they totally miss that last good bit!

I feel in my heart that someone reading this has also just heard bad news and, like the disciples, you are avoiding facing it. He says, 'Don't be afraid, child, trust in my love. I have not given you a spirit that enslaves you to fear but a Spirit of power, love and a sound mind.'

The disciples probably didn't ask Jesus to explain his words because they were too scared. Was it fear that then led them to argue about who was the greatest? When we are afraid, we long to feel better in ourselves, but can seek that comfort in the wrong things. I tend to take refuge in blaming others, but for them it was competitiveness. Jesus knew their hearts, just as he knows ours, but he didn't condemn; instead, he sat with them and, using a little child to demonstrate, explained how true greatness means being willing to be the last, letting others shine and serving rather than being served. In that culture, servants and children were not counted as equal, but Jesus aligned himself with the weak and vulnerable: 'Whoever welcomes one of these little children in my name welcomes me.'

A family who lovingly reached out and welcomed me when I first became a Christian birthed a passion in me to love those who are also weak and struggling. Such love is powerful to transform fear and brokenness.

Lord Jesus, there's so much I don't understand, but thank you that your love is the most important thing. Please fill and anoint me with your Spirit and help me to reach out to the vulnerable in your name.

TRACY WILLIAMSON

Come, follow me

Jesus looked at him and loved him. 'One thing you lack,' he said. 'Go, sell everything you have and give to the poor, and you will have treasure in heaven. Then come, follow me.' (NIV)

I love how Jesus responded to the man who was desperate to inherit eternal life: 'He looked at him and loved him.' Jesus loved the man's hunger for God and his persistence in keeping the commandments, but most of all he loved him as a person. He knew his weakness in making wealth his security, and that was why he told him to give everything up to follow him. He looks at you and me with that same love and deep understanding of our weaknesses.

Sometimes there has to be a radical letting go of certain things in order for us to truly step into freedom. My security was my hatred of the man who had abused me throughout my childhood. I'd always been determined to get my revenge once I was strong enough. It was hard to let that go and walk a different path of forgiveness, but Jesus loved me just as he loved that man. His love melted my heart and empowered me to walk his path.

As the disciples were finding, becoming like Jesus takes a lifetime and the humility to realise that there is always something new to discover, not just about him but about ourselves too. But his character is love and compassion. When people wanted Jesus to bless their children, the disciples rebuked them, thinking he was too important to spend time on dirty kids. But Jesus was indignant with them. He wanted to bless the children and even told the disciples that no one could enter the kingdom of heaven unless they became like a little child. In a culture where children were 'invisible', this was astonishing and once again the disciples had to rethink what they knew and search their own hearts and reactions.

Will I let Jesus' love transform my thinking?

Will you?

Lord, thank you for your love. I choose to follow you in a new way, even in letting go of the things I have held dear. I long for your ways of love to be seen in my life.

TRACY WILLIAMSON

Ministry and discipleship: 1 and 2 Timothy

Michele D. Morrison writes:

Christian ministry is living life in a way that is faithful to Jesus' teaching, while equipping, enabling and encouraging others to do the same. 'I will build my church,' Jesus said, and he builds it through us, as we use the gifts he blesses us with in various ministries. As disciples of Jesus, focusing on his life and teaching is integral to deepening our spiritual lives.

The apostle Paul's letters to his son in the faith, Timothy, are packed with teaching on ministry and discipleship. It is there in the words, and it is also there between the lines, revealed through Paul's relationship to Timothy.

1 Timothy was written shortly after Paul went to Macedonia, leaving Timothy in charge in Ephesus, a city steeped in pagan teaching and the magic arts. Paul, knowing Timothy's timidity, perhaps fears he will wobble and flee, and is intent to impress upon him the need to remain and build up the fledgling church. He reminds him of his calling, gives him a pep talk and then addresses some particular issues.

It's thought that 2 Timothy is the last epistle from Paul before his death. Written from a Roman prison during Nero's reign of terror, this letter shows Paul's intellect and faith mingling with his own human frailty. Lonely and recognising the probability of his imminent execution, he pleads with Timothy to visit him soon, bringing his warm cloak and parchments, probably some of the scriptures. Stripped of everything, in these dire circumstances he craves friendship, physical warmth and spiritual encouragement.

I wonder how Timothy responded to these letters from his spiritual father. Wouldn't it be amazing to see his replies? When I have been separated from my friends and family during testing times, I have depended on my Bible and the emails and prayers I've received. I hope Timothy found a way to reply, because church is at its best when the encouragement and prayers flow in all directions.

Ministry and discipleship are all about believers following hard on the heels of Jesus in faith, walking each other home through mutual encouragement, teaching and love. Let's look at Paul as he shows us how not to just talk the talk, but also walk the walk, right into the kingdom.

Who are you?

Paul, an apostle of Christ Jesus by the command of God our Saviour and of Christ Jesus our hope, To Timothy my true son in the faith: Grace, mercy and peace from God the Father and Christ Jesus our Lord. (NIV)

As a full-time mum, I dreaded the question, 'What do you do?' New acquaintances often turned away, concluding mine was not an interesting life. (Hah!) Ours is a culture that defines people by what they do. A better question would be, '*Who* are you?', and a better answer, 'I am Michele, a disciple of Jesus.'

Paul knew who he was. He opens this letter confidently identifying himself by his calling in Jesus, and he refers to his responsibility to teach 'sound doctrine that conforms to the gospel… which he entrusted to me.'

Knowing our identity is key to robust mental and spiritual health. In a culture where even gender is a matter of choice, many suffer terrible insecurities not knowing who they are. When I was born again, I received a solid assurance of God's love for me, a sinner, and the redeeming love of my Saviour Jesus Christ. I became a disciple, sitting at his feet. I fear there are people in church who don't know this deep love of Jesus, which sets them free to be who he created them to be.

After blessing Timothy with God's grace, mercy and peace, Paul's first instruction is to put a stop to the teaching of false doctrines based on 'endless genealogies'. Genealogies trace generational identity, but as interesting as our ancestral heritage might be, it does not define who we are. If we believe in Christ, we are children of the King. Full stop. The Ephesians were distracted by convoluted discussions based on erroneous teaching. We have to be on our guard: proclaim truth (Jesus) and then focus on and worship him alone.

Confidence in our identity enables disciples to avoid distractions which dilute truth and weaken faith.

Our faith is not based on a fairy tale; it is based on Jesus. Beware of any church whose focus is on a charismatic leader rather than on Jesus, our hope, and on gospel truth.

MICHELE D. MORRISON

Redeemed

I thank Christ Jesus our Lord, who has given me strength, that he considered me trustworthy, appointing me to his service. Even though I was once a blasphemer and a persecutor and a violent man, I was shown mercy. (NIV)

Paul humbly acknowledges that his strength comes from Christ Jesus. The more powerfully Jesus works in and through him, the more aware Paul is of his own sinfulness, and his relationship with Jesus is characterised by faithful service. There is no showboating, no grandstanding, just service on bended knee with eyes and arms raised to the Saviour.

Trying to 'do ministry' or be a faithful disciple in our own strength is crazy. None of us can serve God well without the Holy Spirit empowering us, changing our hearts and transforming our minds. The criterion for discipleship is not a perfect past but a faithful heart trusting for a glorious future while prayerfully serving in an imperfect present. Paul's own serious shortfalls teach that a shady past disqualifies nobody from ministry and discipleship in the kingdom. This is the crux of the gospel: Jesus came to save sinners.

I once went to hear Jonathan Aitken speak on prison reform. Someone remarked to me that she would not walk across the hall to hear him, as he had perjured himself into prison during the Thatcher years. But surely that is the point: yes, he had committed a crime, but Jesus recognised in him a heart which was open to change. In prison, in his darkest moments, Jonathan met Jesus. His life was transformed, and now he is able to lobby and work for prison reform, knowing from personal experience what reform is needed.

A saved sinner encourages others that they aren't beyond the pale. I love the way Paul bursts out in worship and praise when he thinks of God's grace and mercy towards him.

Lord, your grace and mercy extend even to me, a sinner. Thank you for your love. Thank you for your life. Thank you for your Spirit, who lives and works in and through me. Use me, I pray.

MICHELE D. MORRISON

Release the baton

I'm passing this work on to you, my son Timothy. The prophetic word that was directed to you prepared us for this. (MSG)

God blessed Paul with extraordinary gifts, which he used powerfully for the kingdom, and his prayerful relationship with Jesus kept him humble. He knew that Jesus could and would use Timothy's different portfolio of gifts to build his church, but it can be hard to let go of 'your baby'. In passing the baton, Paul had a role model in the self-effacing humility demonstrated by John the Baptist, who recognised when his part in God's plan was nearing an end (see John 3:22–30).

Paul refers to ministry as 'fighting the good fight', and his last epistle, 2 Timothy, ends with his quiet consolation that he had fought it and was ready to move on. Ours is a powerful, deadly enemy, and to wage spiritual warfare effectively we need the gifts of the Spirit. Paul reminds Timothy here of the prophetic word given to him at the beginning of his ministry, which is coming into its fullness now.

Ministering includes encouraging the disciples – the church – as God directs. Far from being stones and mortar, the church is an organic living entity, always changing, but when remaining rooted in Jesus, growing straight and true.

Good foundations are everything. We neglected to put the tent pegs in for the summer marquee we erected to provide shelter from sun and rain during a BBQ. When a storm blew up, the marquee landed like an upturned white elephant, skewered on a fence post in the strawberry patch. Many a church loses their way for lack of sound foundations.

Storms blow up in all of our lives. Some are just part of life, but a wise disciple remembers that we do indeed have a spiritual enemy whose sole objective is to blow us off course. It is a spiritual battle in which we are engaged, but the war was won by Jesus.

Father God, we so easily become spiritually complacent and lazy. Keep us focused on you, rooted in Jesus and eager to use the spiritual gifts you bless us with.

MICHELE D. MORRISON

Lift up holy hands

So then I would like the men everywhere to pray, leading clean lives, without anger or argument. And the same goes for women too. (SOU)

Prayer fuels the church. A basic principle for anyone in a position of Christian ministry is to be a person of prayer.

A book with a testimony that changed my life is Colin Urquhart's *When the Spirit Comes*. Sent as vicar to a dying church in London, Colin prayed. Out of his fervent prayer, revival came in that church. In my experience, we often pay lip service to the critical need for prayer, but don't always bend the knee to God. Thirty years ago, the church in our village was uninspiring. A group of believers got together and prayed, and out of that was born a weekly praise service, Sunday Night Live (SNL). SNL ran for 20 years, birthed at least three ministers and one missionary and revitalised the local church. When Jesus looked around his world, he saw people desperate for the gospel and directed his disciples to pray for helpers to share the good news (Matthew 9:35–38).

I don't know the demographics of your church, but many churches struggle because too few carry the greatest burden of ministry – be it junior church, pastoral care, mission outreach, music worship or other areas of service. Rather than complaining, we should be praying for more helpers to bring in the harvest.

Prayer flows from a loving relationship with God. Why do we so often act as if it is an onerous responsibility rather than an incredible delight to be invited into the presence of the living, almighty God? When we fall in love, we don't need to be instructed to spend time with our beloved. It's the longing of our hearts. As we meet with the Lord in loving fellowship, he is released in power to work his will in the world through us. Prayer is key to all ministry and discipleship. Paul wanted to ensure that Timothy knew this.

Lord Jesus Christ, I worship you. I love you, Lord, and my heart overflows with gratitude for the grace and favour you extend to me and to the whole world. Build your church, we pray.

MICHELE D. MORRISON

Women in ministry (1)

[Martha] had a sister called Mary, who sat at the Lord's feet and was listening to what he said… [Jesus said,] 'Mary has chosen what is better, and it shall not be taken from her.' (SOU)

In Jesus' day, disciples sat at their rabbi's feet, travelled with him and learned. Traditionally, disciples were men, but Jesus had a way of shaking up tradition. We know that Jesus had women in his entourage who financed the ministry, and in this story Luke reveals that Jesus had female disciples. Mary sat at his feet and learned. Martha's irritation with her sister may have stemmed from a deep disquiet that it was not seemly, and that Mary could bring disgrace on the family. Jesus' gentle rebuke reveals that he understood the reason for Martha's anxiety but that being close to him trumped that concern.

I don't think traditional translations of 1 Timothy 2:9–11, our second reading, reflect the way Jesus treated women. He reached out to them and treated them with respect and dignity. He used the Samaritan woman to evangelise men. Paul had women in leadership in his church plants: Lydia, Priscilla, Chloe. In *The Source*, a translation of the New Testament by Dr Ann Nyland, she uses recent papyri discoveries in her approach to the original texts, and certain passages are significantly different. This is one of them, and it is heavily footnoted with information on lexicography, cultural customs and historical situations. I encourage you to get it.

In Kenneth E. Bailey's excellent book, *Jesus through Middle Eastern Eyes*, he devotes a section to Jesus' radical inclusion of women in his coterie of disciples. Ignorance of the nuances of rarely used words has given us translations which have severely limited women's opportunities over the centuries. I realise this is a subject which is highly divisive, but I am passionate that it is not conformity to political correctness, but adherence to Jesus' teaching, that gives women a voice in church and in ministry.

Father God, you have created men and women in your image, and you speak to and through both. Grant us minds open to your teaching and the courage to be bold in embracing our calling.

MICHELE D. MORRISON

Women in ministry (2)

Jesus said to her, 'Mary.' She turned towards him and cried out in Aramaic, 'Rabboni!' (which means 'Teacher'). Jesus said… 'Go instead to my brothers and tell them, "I am ascending to my Father and your Father, to my God and your God."' (NIV)

Jesus told Mary Magdalene to use her voice and tell his brothers that he had risen. She was the first disciple commissioned with the good news of Jesus' resurrection, and she joyfully fulfilled her calling. The disciples didn't believe her, but a few of them didn't ignore her words and ran to check out what she said for themselves.

How does this commission square with a translation of 1 Timothy 2:12 that seems to strip women of the right to speak in a gathering of believers? I don't think it does. In *The Source* (referenced yesterday), Dr Nyland concludes that there is evidence that women were often synagogue leaders, and as such frequently instructed the converts to Judaism. Paul, she believes, is talking to these women in the context of the new teaching of the gospel. These teachers must now become quiet students of the revelations of Jesus before they can resume a teaching position.

'Jesus said to her…' Too often, a paucity of prayer dulls our spiritual ears, and instead of hearing Jesus, we hear tradition. I am grateful to women like Amy Semple McPherson, who defied convention in Los Angeles in the 1920s; the Foursquare Church came out of the teaching Jesus gave to her, bringing renewed interest in the gifts of the Holy Spirit.

I am not trying to stir things up or undermine anyone's deeply held convictions, but for myself, I believe that our identity in Christ as his daughters, and the way Jesus himself used his female disciples to spread the word, illustrate that God calls who he calls into ministries of all types, and as humble seekers of truth we are to listen and prayerfully weigh up what we hear from whoever is preaching or teaching.

Father God, give me a clear understanding of the commission you are giving to me. May I be inspired, taught and equipped by your Holy Spirit to faithfully follow you.

MICHELE D. MORRISON

Role models

I'm writing this letter so you'll know how things ought to go in God's household, this God-alive church, bastion of truth. (MSG)

Paul defines the character qualities required for leadership in the church, which he describes as God's household, the pillar and foundation of the truth. He reminds Timothy of the awesome truth expressed in what is thought to have been an early church hymn. Setting truth to music is a powerful way to proclaim and internalise the gospel.

Paul affirms the teaching power of role models. Actions speak louder than words. Behind all of our actions is the inspiration of the life of Jesus, our ultimate role model. He was perfect and holy, and yet fully human. He spent whole nights on the hills in prayer, had a heart for the poor and the marginalised, and reached out to the hurting. Guided by the Spirit, he only did what he saw his Father in heaven do. As disciples and ministers, followers and leaders, we are called to model his characteristics to a watching world. We can only do this through the power of the Holy Spirit.

It's so encouraging to read in Revelation 2:1–7 that the once-rowdy Ephesian church is commended by Jesus for their deeds, their hard work and their perseverance. Timid Timothy, encouraged and taught by his mentor Paul, and inspired by the Spirit, succeeded in modelling a bold life of faith based on truth. The church grew up, but in its greater maturity lost its passion. Leaders need maturity, but they must never lose their deep love for Jesus. It's a tricky balance but not impossible to achieve. We only need look at Paul to see an example of one whose passion was fuelled by his relationship with Jesus.

In ancient Greek, 'church' referred to people gathered for a purpose, not necessarily religious. Our purpose as church is to model truth in a world confused by untruthful alternatives.

Tell out my soul, the greatness of his name! Jesus, the author and perfecter of my faith, thank you that you are truth. On you I build my life. In you I live it out. For you I shout for joy!

MICHELE D. MORRISON

Keep training!

Exercise daily in God – no spiritual flabbiness, please! Workouts in the gymnasium are useful, but a disciplined life in God is far more so, making you fit both today and forever. (MSG)

Paul prescribes spiritual strength gained through regular study, and teaching through words, actions and attitudes. Again, he reminds Timothy of the prophetic gift of ministry he received through the laying on of hands. Oddly, it is easy to neglect spiritual gifts, perhaps disbelieving our own worthiness. It's not about how we feel, though, but who God declares us to be: his daughters. In Jesus, we are worthy.

It is easy to be too busy in the world to spend time in the word. Memorising scripture is a discipline we neglect to our cost. I am rubbish at it, but I have learned a good chunk of the opening of John's gospel. Recently, I had a painful hour in the dentist's surgery, and as my dentist hammered, I focused on Jesus by mentally repeating what I remembered. It was tremendously comforting!

As the recent concept of 'fake news' has taken hold, encouraging distrust of leaders and news sources alike, some prefer to believe tweets or Facebook posts rather than official statements from government sources. Non-believers hear about Jesus' claim to be the truth and cynically ask, as did Pontius Pilate, 'What is truth?' The antidote to the poison of deception is the elixir of the word of God. We need to memorise it.

We are in a spiritual battle, and the enemy's tactics are not always 'in your face'; sometimes they are subtle. If we are to be effective contenders for Jesus, we need to put on our armour (Ephesians 6), and to be walking through each day alert to his presence and sensitive to his Spirit. Godliness isn't served up on a tray; we have to train. Many of us go to the gym to keep our bodies in good shape, but spiritual exercising is even more important.

Lord, help me to reset my priorities so that you are always first in my life. Put my spiritual sensitivities on high alert so that I am not deceived. Help me to memorise your word.

MICHELE D. MORRISON

That's what family does

Do not verbally attack an older man, but encourage him as a father, and younger men as brothers, older women as mothers, and younger women as sisters, with a great deal of holiness. (SOU)

I was driving two of my grandchildren to our house when Felicity, aged three, piped up, 'Thank you, Grandma, for letting us use your car.' After I replied, she continued, quoting my husband: 'He said that's what family does.' Young children are watching and listening all the time, and learning important lessons.

Paul sees the church as family, and as he explores various relationships in this chapter, he encourages Timothy to make sure that church looks after its own. He is at pains to ensure that destitute widows are cared for. There was a cultural expectation that the dowry given at marriage would be kept apart from the husband's property, possibly invested, and at his death the widow would receive it back. That was about as far as the welfare state went in first-century tradition, but not every widow did receive her dowry back. So Paul is encouraging the church to look out for those in need within the fellowship of believers. Pastoral care is a characteristic of Christian ministry and discipleship, and has been since earliest times.

There is a reminder here to value the older generation, showing them gratitude in a practical way. How does your church treat older people? Are you more focused on youth and children's work, or is there an active ministry to all generations? We sometimes bring some of our older friends to our home for an old-fashioned afternoon tea. They are grateful, but so are we, as we listen with delight to reminiscences of their long lives and hear some of their experiences and insights.

Paul's instructions on the way we should treat church leaders are worth thinking about, too. We can too easily roast the preacher for Sunday lunch instead of praying for and encouraging her or him.

Father God, thank you for the picture of church as family. Keep us from being dysfunctional, and help us to value and treat each other with kindness, love and respect.

MICHELE D. MORRISON

The good life

Lust for money brings trouble and nothing but trouble… Run for your life from all this. Pursue a righteous life – a life of wonder, faith, love, steadiness, courtesy. Run hard and fast in the faith. (MSG)

It takes rock-solid faith to resist the powerful seductions of the world, especially the lust for money. Some televangelists have betrayed Jesus, using 'godliness [as] a means to financial gain' (NIV) and amassing fortunes for themselves. Paul's teaching reveals that this is not a modern phenomenon.

Money is an idol of this age, as it was in Paul's age. True disciples, Paul teaches, know that real riches are found in Jesus. As we pursue Jesus, the cheap tawdriness of money and what it buys is revealed. Paul highlights the upside-down nature of the gospel: that we are rich when we give away our time serving others and our wealth helping those in need. Extravagant generosity brings everlasting rewards as well as peace in this lifetime.

Peace. More and more people admit to being 'nervous wrecks', eaten up by anxiety and robbed of peace. Someone I know has built a financially successful career, motivated by what money can buy. As his firm grew, he acquired high-end cars: Porsches, a Lamborghini and a Mercedes. Though he has reached retirement age, his desire to live near the water has compelled him to buy an expensive home, though he already has a lovely place. He has been seduced by the goodies money can buy, and works 24/7 to finance his acquisitions. Is that life?

Fight the good fight of the faith, Paul tells Timothy. Our enemy is wily and full of clever tricks to lure us away from God. We are all tempted by the mirages of worldly wealth, and in order to stay on track we need to live close to God. It takes energy, effort and courage. It requires self-discipline and a willingness to prioritise time with God so that we can recognise the devil's schemes and run from them.

Father God, help me to hold money and possessions lightly as I run after you. Enable me to loosen my grip and become an example of extravagant generosity.

MICHELE D. MORRISON

Famous last words

I thank God, whom I serve, as my ancestors did, with a clear conscience, as night and day I constantly remember you in my prayers. (NIV)

This intensely personal final letter of Paul exudes inspirational encouragement to his much-loved son in the faith. Grace, mercy and peace, he prays, reminding himself, as he faces death, of the promise of life in Jesus. The powerful disciple is a person of constant prayer, which starts with thanksgiving.

At Stonehenge, the builders engineered the stone circle to capture the first rays of the sun at the solstices, believing there to be power in that alignment. I believe that a thankful heart aligns us with the will of God so that when we pray our needs, the power flashes forth. This doesn't mean that the answer 'yes' always flashes forth, but being aligned with the powerful presence of God is what prayer is all about, entrusting him as the source of love to act in the best possible way in every situation.

Paul could be excused if he had written to Timothy with a desperate prayer request: that he would be released from the horrors of a Roman prison. He could have justified such a prayer. He still hadn't been to Spain, where he wanted to evangelise. But his constant prayer is for Timothy, of whom he is so proud. His pride isn't in Timothy's accomplishments but in his faith.

One of my sons pulled back from faith during his teens. After university he lived and worked in Tanzania, where he recommitted his life to Jesus. The letter I received from him that Christmas telling me the story is one of the best gifts I've ever received. My prayers for him had been pretty constant, so I love the praise inherent in Paul's recollection that Timothy's faith came from his grandmother and his mother. The church family has a huge privilege to pray for our children, with thanksgiving.

It's our privilege as church to pray for our own individual families but also the young children and youth in our midst, that in this dark world they will be bold and strong in faith.

MICHELE D. MORRISON

More power, Lord

Fan into flame the gift of God, which is in you through the laying on of my hands. For the Spirit God gave us does not make us timid, but gives us power, love and self-discipline. (NIV)

In 2018, Greece, Canada and many US states, including California, were burning. These wildfires, firefighters said, were more aggressive than usual, throwing up fire tornadoes which suddenly surrounded and engulfed fleeing victims.

I am from California. One of my sons studied at Bethel in Redding, where one of the fiercest fires raged and where half the city had to be evacuated. The church there known as 'Bethel' is a church on fire for God, and it was surrounded by a physical fire of apocalyptic proportions.

Paul couples his exhortation to Timothy to fan into flames the gift of God with a reminder that the Spirit in us is one of power. When we stir up and use the gifts God gives us, we can expect to find ourselves in a spiritual firestorm where we will need faith and courage, love, self-discipline and power.

Paul is writing this letter to Timothy while he is in chains in a Roman prison. He is in the heart of the firestorm as the enemy seeks to silence his voice. He is desperate for Timothy to breathe the Spirit deep into his being, douse any fear or timidity and step out in faith in the power of the Spirit.

I love the story of the earliest days of the church, when Peter and John were released from prison and the gathered disciples prayed, not that they would be delivered from persecution, or that the rulers would soften up, but rather, 'Now Lord, consider their threats and enable your servants to speak your word with great boldness. Stretch out your hand to heal and perform signs and wonders through the name of your holy servant Jesus' (Acts 4:29–30).

More love, more power, Lord. Fan into flame the gift of God.

God has given each of us gifts for the growth of the kingdom. Fan them into flame, and pray for our persecuted sisters and brothers, that they will be filled with the Spirit's power and love.

MICHELE D. MORRISON

On fire for Jesus

There will be terrible times in the last days. People will be lovers of themselves, lovers of money… lovers of pleasure rather than lovers of God – having a form of godliness but denying its power. (NIV)

My encounter with the Holy Spirit, when I was born again, sparked a godly firestorm which raged within my spirit, burning the dross and cleansing the vessel (me) to receive the gift of God, his Holy Spirit. The friend with me could feel the heat emanating from my body, and I could certainly feel the heat in the depths of my soul, and I was changed forever.

If the church is to make a difference for Jesus during these perilous times in which we live, we need to be serious about our faith and on fire for our King. Paul thought the world was nearing the end times, as do many in the church today. Maybe it is; maybe it isn't. For the sake of the gospel… for the sake of those who don't yet know the salvation of King Jesus… we the church need to focus, work hard and lead disciplined, pure lives, strong in grace and trusting in God to transform others. Living out the lives of true disciples is a powerful ministry in itself, speaking volumes to a world cynical and sickened by the hypocrisy of many leaders in society and the church. Paul reminds Timothy that he knows the right teaching and he's seen Paul's lifestyle, and on those he should model his life and ministry. And finally, he praises the power of scripture to equip every believer to live out the gospel.

We the church can be equipped with the power of the word and the power of the Spirit, and live bold, naturally supernatural lives in expectation of seeing God work miracles all around us. In and through him, we can change the world.

Be 'loved up, prayed up, filled up', and go out there in his power as his disciples and ministers, full of hope and confidence that God wins in the end.

MICHELE D. MORRISON

The end is in sight

Proclaim the Message with intensity; keep on your watch. Challenge, warn, and urge your people. Don't ever quit. Just keep it simple. (MSG)

'Just keep it simple.' I am no theologian, but I love the Lord and I ask him regularly to speak to me through circumstances and through nature as well as through his word and in prayer – and he does. When he does, he keeps it simple. I write much of what he says in this way in my blog, and some have expressed surprise that I see lessons in simple things. It's my language of love with my Saviour. I don't like getting tangled up in theological debates.

I'm not discounting the importance of theological understanding and discourse, but I have noticed, as I've read these two letters intensively over these past days, how often Paul encourages Timothy not to get embroiled in discussions and words that end in quarrels. How many church splits, I wonder, could be avoided if instead of debating issues, we sat together and invited the Spirit to burn out the dross within us and speak to us in simple terms?

Paul was impassioned that the gospel be shared throughout the world. Jesus hated the lukewarm attitudes of the church in Laodicea (Revelation 3:15–16). Preachers should be passionate about God. At the wedding of Prince Harry and Meghan Markle in 2018, millions around the world were astonished at the passion of the preacher, Bishop Michael Curry. They expected a ho-hum homily which might or might not contain a few words of wisdom for the couple. Instead, they heard the good news of God's love, proclaimed with intensity.

The end of this letter is a moving tribute to the church of which Paul was a part. He has messages for his co-workers and news of the health – physical and spiritual – of others, all whom he names. Through Paul's ministry in the Spirit, the church emerged as a living legacy to the Lord's love.

O Lord, I thank you for Paul's life, for his faithfulness and his courage, his strength and his wisdom, and the weakness that kept him leaning, always leaning, on you. May I be the same.

MICHELE D. MORRISON

Servant-hearted: following the master who serves

Hannah Fytche writes:

Servant-heartedness is a quality Christians often talk about. We're called to 'serve' God and 'serve' others: to use our time and gifts to love those around us.

That serving will look different for each of us, depending on our individual personalities. There are so many ways that we can serve: as God's church, we are one body made up of many parts, all of which serve each other differently. Serving is not about how many church rotas or teams each of us is on: it is not about *doing* or about completing a checklist of tasks and performing numerous duties.

Serving is rather about a way of *being*: being ourselves. We serve well when we are being ourselves in the best way possible, because God has made and given each of us gifts and strengths to serve in his church and world. Notice the community around you and ask: 'What do I have that I can give? How can I, with my individual gifts, weaknesses, strengths and passions, love those around me?'

You see, serving comes from the heart. It comes from the heart which rests in God: a heart set free and given confidence to live, follow and serve, exactly as it's been made. The way our hearts are set free is by God himself, in Jesus Christ. Even more extraordinary is the fact that Jesus sets us free to serve by *coming to serve us first*.

Imagine that! The creator of the universe, of stars and oceans, the one who holds truth in his hands – come to serve us! He came to set us free from what holds us back from being with him and from being ourselves.

Over the next 14 days, we are going to get to know this master who serves. We'll reflect on passages from Isaiah which describe Jesus as the suffering, victorious servant. We'll read a story from John and a hymn written to the Philippians, focusing on how Jesus came and served his people, and showing us how we can respond to him. Finally, passages from Romans and Galatians will illuminate the freedom, life and fruit that God promises to bring as we follow Jesus and grow in servant-heartedness.

Let's pray as we begin: for Jesus to show us how he serves and loves us, and for our hearts to find in him their rest and confidence to serve.

61

Here is my servant

'Here is my servant, whom I uphold, my chosen one in whom I delight; I will put my Spirit on him, and he will bring justice to the nations.'
(NIV)

These words are old, first written in a time of great pain, tension and suffering. The people of Israel, God's people, were abandoned to their enemies. What hope had they left?

Into this hopelessness, Isaiah prophesies. He lifts his eyes from the specific situation of exile to gaze upon the larger purposes of God – and he receives promise of a 'servant' that God will send, one whom God has chosen and in whom God's Spirit will rest and bring justice to the nations. During injustice and loss, God promises a servant who will bring justice. He whispers hope.

Here we are, thousands of years later, and those whispers of hope have become shouts and roars for us today. This is because we have a New Testament perspective: the 'servant' that God promised in Isaiah's prophecy has come. He has walked among his people. He has died and risen to life for them, in order to deliver nations and peoples and the whole wide world from injustice and pain. He is Jesus.

If you read the story of Jesus' baptism in Matthew 3:13–17, you'll see that he is indeed the one promised by Isaiah. At Jesus' baptism, God affirms him as the one that he has chosen, in whom he delights and on whom his Spirit rests. 'This is my Son,' God says, 'whom I love; with him I am well pleased.' Here is my servant, God promises, and he will bring justice to the nations.

Father, thank you that you spoke words of promise and hope, and sent Jesus as a servant to fulfil them and bring justice and life. Give me hope, as I am a part of this, your larger purpose and story.

HANNAH FYTCHE

Tender in justice

'A bruised reed he will not break, and a smouldering wick he will not snuff out.' (NIV)

'Here is my servant,' God has said, 'and he will bring justice.' God continues by describing this servant and his justice. 'A bruised reed he will not break, and a smouldering wick he will not snuff out.'

Isn't this beautiful? It's so tender and gentle. Anything that has a glimmer of life Jesus, God's servant, will treat with deepest tenderness. He will bring it back to life; life is his justice.

Even a bruised reed – a thin, papery leaf, beaten and bent a little – even this he will not break. I have broken many reeds. I have broken literal plants: the silvery, grassy kind that grow alongside country lanes at hand height, easy to snap by the dozen.

I have broken metaphorical plants, too: I have snapped fragile stems of hope in different situations; I have hurt people with careless, hurried words spoken before listening. I have treated myself with unforgiveness and pressure, too, breaking my own bruised reed when I should have cared and rested a little more.

We all have done this: bruised reeds we have broken.

Yet Jesus will not break a bruised, fragile reed. He will care for it, heal the bruises and make it whole. He will give it the tender rest it needs. He will kindle new life.

He will kindle new life: even a smouldering wick he will not snuff out. Picture a candle on the verge of burnout, the wick glowing that final red glow. It would be easy to wet your fingers and pinch it out – but this is not what Jesus will do. He will be a servant to it, tenderly breathing on it so that it burns bright once more.

Such life from death is the justice God's servant will bring, tenderly and faithfully, 'till he establishes justice on earth'.

Jesus, show me your gentle care when I am bruised. Show me where you would like me to bring your justice: the bruised reeds that need healing; the smouldering wicks that need fanning into flame.

HANNAH FYTCHE

Hidden for splendour

He made my mouth like a sharpened sword, in the shadow of his hand he hid me; he made me into a polished arrow and concealed me in his quiver. He said to me, 'You are my servant, Israel, in whom I will display my splendour.' (NIV)

Here, the perspective of Isaiah's prophecy shifts from the third to the first person: the servant describes himself. He portrays himself as sharp and poised, hidden in God's hand and made ready to display God's splendour.

It is quite surprising that God chooses to make his splendour known through a servant – one lower than him. Yet this is what God promised to do. He chose his servant and hid him in the shadow of his hand. Like a polished arrow concealed in the quiver, waiting for the moment to be sent out. His mouth – representing his words and speech – was sharpened like a sword (see Hebrews 4:12). He's ready to display God's splendour.

In verse 3, God's servant is called 'Israel'. This is the first application of Isaiah's prophecy: God's chosen people Israel would be his servant among the nations. The Old Testament tells stories of Israelites (for example, David) becoming God's unlikely servants.

As New Testament events unfolded, prophecies like Isaiah's were applied to Jesus: 'Jesus' can now be read instead of 'Israel' in verse 3. Jesus, seemingly an ordinary carpenter's son, is the unlikely servant in whom God displays his splendour. We begin to see *him* as the one held in the shadow of God's hand, made ready for the precise moment he would be born in Bethlehem. He was held for splendour, purposed by God.

There is a third application of this prophecy. Christians, those who are in Jesus, become 'Israel'; because of Jesus, we become God's people in whom he will display his splendour. It is so unlikely: how many of us would expect to be chosen for such a privilege?

This is the brilliant, surprising joy of being called to be servant-hearted towards God: we are hidden for splendour.

Father, thank you that you choose unexpected people to be your servants and to display your splendour. Help me to see and respond to the ways you hide me in your hands and prepare me for your purposes.

HANNAH FYTCHE

Strengthened in weakness

But I said, 'I have laboured in vain; I have spent my strength for nothing at all. Yet what is due me is in the Lord's hand, and my reward is with my God.' (NIV)

How this verse resonates with those of us who labour and are heavy-burdened – which, I guess, is all of us. Have you felt worn-through and exhausted, close to tears and wondering if you have the strength to keep going?

As I write these words, I am in the midst of a pressured time. I am finishing university while looking for a job and a place to live; I am also balancing a busy church and college life, figuring out my place in the midst of change.

It's hard in these times to see what fruit is coming from all the effort. I am sure you will have encountered similar seasons, times when you've laboured hard for what is good, only to be left wondering what is coming of it all. You're tired, and you're questioning whether God is still there.

It's so comforting to see that God's servant, prophesied in Isaiah and fulfilled in Jesus, felt those same feelings. I think of Jesus in the garden of Gethsemane (Matthew 26:36–46), praying that the heavy task ahead of him might be removed. He's worn out, so exhausted and fearful that his sweat is like drops of blood.

The words in Isaiah 49 show God's answer to such prayers: he transforms his servant so that he can say, 'Yet what is due me is in the Lord's hand, and my reward is with my God.' In the midst of fear and weariness, the servant's faith is renewed – his weakness is transformed to strength. Jesus stands up from his prayers in the garden to face his betrayers, knowing that the labour of death ahead of him will not be fruitless.

When we feel that same weariness from doing good, we can look to Jesus' example. We can pray and see our faith renewed.

Father, when we feel weary and heavy-burdened, help us to come to you and see our faith renewed. Thank you that Jesus prayed and you strengthened him for the task ahead.

HANNAH FYTCHE

Light in darkness

He says: 'It is too small a thing for you to be my servant to restore the tribes of Jacob and bring back those of Israel I have kept. I will also make you a light for the Gentiles, that my salvation may reach to the ends of the earth.' (NIV)

We've seen three characteristics of God's servant Jesus: he is tender in justice, hidden for splendour and strengthened in weakness. Now we zoom out to view the wider narrative of God's purposes which are to be accomplished by his servant.

God's purpose is restoration. It is light in darkness.

Light in darkness: a candle held up in the middle of the night, a flame flickering bright and brighter until the darkness is overcome. Light shines in the darkness, and the darkness will never overcome it.

This light is salvation, restoration, life. It is God's goodness illuminating the places of the world that are hurting and broken. It leads people out of darkness – out of shame, fear, waywardness – into the kingdom of God's glorious light, where all is made whole.

This is why God sends his servant. He has a vision of the world restored to what it was created to be. We can claim this salvation for our own: how have you seen Jesus' light in your life? How has he led and guided you out of darkness, making you more whole?

Yet we do not only claim this salvation for ourselves. God's purpose of restoration and light in darkness is for the whole world, for every person and place; it is not only promised for the Israelites, God's particular people at the time of Isaiah's prophecy. God's salvation is for the Gentiles, too, and it will reach the ends of the earth. God intends to catch all people up in his love and glory.

Jesus' servant-heartedness is outward-looking. He will look to the ends of the earth, working to bring his overcoming, life-giving light to every corner of creation. Where have you seen Jesus' light bringing life? Are there any places where you can serve him in this way?

Father, thank you that your purposes are for all people. Show me where you are bringing light and love in my life and in the whole world. May I serve you by sharing Jesus, bringing light to every place I go.

HANNAH FYTCHE

Suffering in faith

'I offered my back to those who beat me, my cheeks to those who pulled out my beard; I did not hide my face from mocking and spitting. Because the Sovereign Lord helps me, I will not be disgraced. Therefore have I set my face like flint, and I know I will not be put to shame.' (NIV)

This is another part of Isaiah written in the voice of the servant. It is vivid and confrontational, painting an intense portrait of the cost Jesus took upon himself as God's servant, in order to fulfil God's purposes for his people. It is in his suffering, his pain and his humiliation that he serves God.

An old hymn, adapted as a modern worship song, has these lyrics: 'See from his head, his hands, his feet/Sorrow and love, flow mingled down/Did e'er such love and sorrow meet/Or thorns compose so rich a crown?' (Isaac Watts, 1707).

They are beautiful words, capturing the pain of Jesus' sacrifice and the love that motivates him. God's purposes are light in darkness, a display of his splendour and life for all people and creation. It is by his costly love and sorrow that he brings these purposes into the world.

With the vision of light and life for creation set before him, Jesus endures beating, mocking, spitting and crucifixion. He knows that God will bring forth his splendour, and he has faith that ultimately he will not be put to shame. Jesus takes up his cross and endures, held safe in the hands of his Father.

Sometimes, in our own servant-heartedness towards God, we will encounter suffering and pain. There will be frustrations. There will be moments when darkness threatens to overwhelm us or situations in which we are serving and living. It will not always be easy – God never promised that it would be.

Yet he did promise that he would always be with us. He has promised that his children will never be put to shame. We can have faith, like Jesus did, as we endure to serve God through troubling times. We are held safe in the hands of our Father.

Father, sometimes I find myself struggling as I seek to serve you and follow the path you have set out before me. Hold me in the midst of this pain and trouble, and strengthen my faith and confidence in you.

HANNAH FYTCHE

Here I am, your servant

Jesus knew that the Father had put all things under his power, and that he had come from God and was returning to God; so he got up from the meal, took off his outer clothing, and wrapped a towel around his waist. (NIV)

Jesus knew. He knew his power as one who was from God and returning to him. He knew he had been hidden in the shadow of God's hand, and that he would return to God in splendour when his task was completed.

Jesus knew – and he knelt down.

This mighty one from God, God's own servant, kneels. He strips off his clothes and wraps a cloth around his waist.

His disciples crowd around him, their feet in open sandals stinking to high heaven, having been coated in the dust and muck of the road. Their eyes widen in disbelief as they realise that Jesus is kneeling ready to wash their feet. Another servant more suited to the status of the task would not be summoned: this master they'd followed, the one who had performed miracles and wonders, was showing himself to be their servant.

Can you imagine? What a holy, humbling moment it must have been, to see the holy one washing their feet. Imagine yourself in the shoes (sandals) of those disciples. Jesus kneels to wash your feet. He is the master who serves, and he has come to serve you.

Whatever you bring with you, whatever shame or happiness, brokenness or pride, joy or loneliness, whatever it is that you've picked up on your life's journey – whatever coats your feet – Jesus, who came from God and returned to him and who even now sits at God's right hand, kneels to wash your feet.

This story from John's gospel shows that Jesus fulfils Isaiah's prophecies of God's servant. He kneels to wash your feet and sets you free – as we'll see. For now, keep imagining yourself into the story. Hear Jesus whispering to you, 'Here I am, the master who serves.'

Jesus, thank you that you knew that you came from God and would return to him – and that you humbled yourself to wash your disciples' feet. Help me to see your unbelievable servant-heartedness.

HANNAH FYTCHE

Behold him

He made himself nothing by taking the very nature of a servant, being made in human likeness. And being found in appearance as a man, he humbled himself by becoming obedient to death — even death on a cross! (NIV)

Alternating with our reflections on the foot-washing story in John will be some reflections on the hymn in Paul's letter to the Philippians. This hymn was probably sung by the earliest Christian communities as they worshipped Jesus, telling the story of his death, resurrection and exaltation.

When we think about Jesus' death and resurrection, we often like to skip over that first, dark part – the death – and move on to celebrating the bright, brilliant victory of the resurrection. Yet this hymn in Philippians invites us first to stop and sit with the death, the cross, before we move on. It invites us to consider Jesus' humility.

This is important for so many reasons – one of which is that humility is at the heart of Jesus' servant-heartedness. Yesterday we saw Jesus' humility as he knelt to wash his disciples' feet. Today we see it again: Jesus emptied himself, making himself nothing, becoming a servant in human likeness. God himself took on flesh and humbled himself in obedience, even to death. In servant-heartedness, he allowed himself to be betrayed and mocked, setting his face like flint and offering his back to those who beat him (as we saw in that vivid Isaiah passage a couple of days ago). He humbled himself to be led to the darkest moment of crucifixion – and all to serve his people, to give us life.

Behold him. Behold Jesus, God's servant, the master who serves. Behold the wounds in his hands and feet, his side: see the marks of the cross that he bore for you. Be amazed by his servant-heartedness, borne of love – sit with that dark night of the cross, and find that at the centre of it is a dazzling, bright glimpse of Jesus' love for you.

Jesus, you revealed your great love in your humble obedience. Thank you that you love us so much you offered yourself as a servant. Give me the grace to behold the cross, and see there the depths of your servant-hearted love.

HANNAH FYTCHE

Receive him

'No,' said Peter, 'you shall never wash my feet.' Jesus answered, 'Unless I wash you, you have no part with me.' 'Then, Lord,' Simon Peter replied, 'not just my feet but my hands and my head as well!' (NIV)

Jesus became like a servant. He knelt to wash his disciples' feet, and he was led to the cross. Jesus is the master who serves: we have begun to behold him as such. Now we continue to respond, looking at how one of his disciples reacted to him as he knelt to wash his feet.

Peter's first reaction is this: 'No, you shall never wash my feet.' Peter sees Jesus as master: he has confessed Jesus to be the holy one of God (John 6:66–69). Because of this, Peter tries to refuse Jesus' humble servant-heartedness. He cannot grasp how being a servant is at the core of who Jesus is as the master. Surely the holy one should not stoop to wash his stinking feet? Surely he should not die for him?

Have you ever had a similar reaction to Jesus? Sometimes it can be hard to let yourself be washed and made whole by Jesus. We think that we have to make ourselves 'clean' or 'good enough' because surely Jesus, God's holy one, cannot look us in the eye and still love us and heal our hurting places. He is too good, too holy, too majestic for that.

Like Peter, it can be easy to distance yourself from Jesus because he is holy, he is God. But this is the utter joy of the gospel: Jesus, precisely as God's holy one, makes himself close to us by serving us. Receiving him as he does so is the only way to be made whole and free.

We see this in Jesus' gentle, corrective words to Peter: 'Unless I wash you, you have no part with me.' He shows Peter that receiving Jesus as the master who serves, however paradoxical this seems, is essential for knowing him, for being made whole.

Jesus, help us to receive you as the master who serves, the holy one who chooses to make himself close to us. Show us the grace, the gift, of your servant-heartedness, and the joy of this gospel message.

HANNAH FYTCHE

Know him

Therefore God exalted him to the highest place and gave him the name that is above every name, that at the name of Jesus every knee should bow, in heaven and on earth and under the earth, and every tongue acknowledge that Jesus Christ is Lord, to the glory of God the Father. (NIV)

Behold him as the master who serves. Receive his servant-heartedness towards you as the only way to be with him. Know him as the one at whose name every knee will bow and every tongue confess that he is Lord.

This is a spectacular image, woven not only into this ancient hymn in Philippians but also into many modern worship songs and hymns. It expresses both faith and hope: the confession of faith that Jesus Christ is Lord, and the hope that one day everyone will claim this joyful confession as their own. The whole of heaven and earth will bow before him.

What would it look like for everyone – everyone we know, everyone we don't know, our own selves, the whole of creation – to know that Jesus, the servant-king, is Lord? What beauty would arise out of this confession?

Knowing Jesus as the servant-hearted, exalted Lord allows me to be free. The world doesn't rest on my shoulders; it rests on his. My life doesn't have to be shaped around striving for approval or affection; it can be shaped around knowing Jesus and his love for me. He washed my feet clean; there's nothing more that I need do. I am free.

My life can be built on knowing Jesus as the one who wept in the garden of Gethsemane and who was strengthened by his Father to go to the cross anyway, in servant-hearted humility and love. I am loved: there is nothing I can do to make God love me more, or less.

This is the joy of making this confession. Reflect on what difference this confession of faith has made to your life. What does it mean, in your everyday living and being, that Jesus made himself like a servant out of love for you?

Jesus, even your name is powerful. At it every knee will bow, in gratitude, freedom and hope. May you and your sacrifice be the foundation for my life, allowing me to turn away from earning approval and instead follow you.

HANNAH FYTCHE

Follow him

'Now that I, your Lord and Teacher, have washed your feet, you also should wash one another's feet. I have set you an example that you should do as I have done for you.' (NIV)

Your feet are washed clean; you are close to Jesus, God's servant. Now, he invites you to go and wash others' feet. It is only after we have received and known Jesus as servant that he then calls us to serve. Our service is rooted in being served. We serve because he has served us and given us everything we need: our service isn't rooted in an attempt to prove ourselves or our worth. We love because he first loved us.

What does this love and service look like? What does it mean to wash one another's feet?

The key to envisioning 'servant-heartedness' is Jesus' example. Think back over our reflections on servant-heartedness. What example has Jesus set us?

In Isaiah, we saw that he is described as tender in justice, hidden for splendour, strengthened in weakness, light in darkness and suffering in faith. In John and Philippians, we have seen his acts of great humility, overflowing from his love for his people.

These are all facets of Jesus' example of servant-heartedness. Do any of them particularly resonate with you? Are there any that you'd like to grow in, or learn to embody in your life and service?

At the moment, the imagery of light in darkness jumps out at me. I'm learning to look at the darkness of our world for what it really is, and to light a candle against it anyway. I'm learning what it means to follow Jesus' example by illuminating the dark and hard places for people: learning how to bring light and hope to different situations, through listening and encouraging, praying and practically helping people.

Pray that God would lead you as you follow him, showing you how to grow in servant-heartedness after the example of Jesus.

Jesus, thank you that my serving is rooted in your love for me. Thank you that I don't have to prove myself to you. Show me how you want me to grow in servant-heartedness as I follow you.

HANNAH FYTCHE

Be set free

Thanks be to God that, though you used to be slaves to sin, you have come to obey from your heart the pattern of teaching that has now claimed your allegiance. You have been set free from sin and have become slaves to righteousness. (NIV)

When we follow Jesus, we are set free. This is because we become 'slaves to righteousness': we live according to God's commands, his 'pattern of teaching' which gives freedom and joy.

At the end of my undergraduate degree, I was considering what I would do next. I had some conversations and times of prayer that made everything click into place: from many options, it was narrowed down to one. Even more amazing was that my fear and scepticism about the future was transformed to overwhelming joy, as I trusted God.

I can only attribute that joy to God being with me, leading me. As I became open to following him – to being servant-hearted towards him – he affirmed and encouraged me. I was free to follow him and live openly and happily.

Sometimes it feels like a challenge to discern where God is leading us. But we need to remember that God's will for us is not a particular place or job, relationship or decision. Rather, his will for us is 'to obey from your heart the pattern of teaching that has now claimed your allegiance'. It is to know the master we serve and to follow, from our hearts, the pattern he lays out before us.

This is so freeing! The pattern God sets for us is not a mystery: it is laid out before us in the Bible, and God writes it on our hearts when we pray. We don't have to come up with the roadmap ourselves; rather, we are free to follow where God calls us.

This is what I found at the end of my undergraduate years: my joy overflowed from knowing that I could walk in the pattern that God had already set out. I was serving him, and I was free.

Jesus, thank you that you have given us a pattern to live by, and that this pattern – rather than any specific plan – is your will for us. Help me to listen to your teaching and become servant-hearted towards you.

HANNAH FYTCHE

Gain life

What benefit did you reap at that time from the things you are now ashamed of? Those things result in death! But now that you have been set free from sin and have become slaves of God, the benefit you reap leads to holiness, and the result is eternal life. (NIV)

It is not only freedom that we receive from God as we serve him; we also gain life.

Did you notice that we gain life *before* death as well as life *after* death? We do have the promise of life after death with God – and that is incredible, but it is not the totality of the gift. The gift of God is 'eternal' life': life stretching into eternity both ways. God gives us the promise of life in the future, but he also gives us the transforming promise of life in the *present*. Our lives can be transformed as we serve him: we can have shame-free, full and meaningful life right now, here in the midst of everything.

Instead of fear, God gives us confidence. Instead of shame, God gives us forgiveness and healing. Instead of despair, God gives us joy – joy not contingent on circumstances but rooted in the promises of God. Instead of succumbing to lies, we can live in the truth. We can look darkness directly in the face and hold up a candle against it anyway: this is the confidence God gives us.

Our servant-heartedness overflows from this promise of whole, confident, deeply joyful life. Having eternal life means that we don't have to feel obligated to serve: we can choose to serve as God calls us. It means that we don't have to prove ourselves through serving: we can rest when we need to.

With the sure and steady promise of God as our foundation, we can take risks in our serving, seeking to repair what seems impossibly broken. We can seek to bring real healing and wholeness to the world, witnessing that our Jesus loves, saves and longs to give the whole world freedom and life – no matter the cost or circumstance.

Jesus, how incredible are your promises! Transform my life so that I live in the freedom and confidence that comes from knowing you. May this overflow into my serving, so that more people may witness your grace.

HANNAH FYTCHE

The fruit of the Spirit

The fruit of the Spirit is love, joy, peace, forbearance, kindness, goodness, faithfulness, gentleness and self-control… Those who belong to Christ Jesus have crucified the flesh with its passions and desires. Since we live by the Spirit, let us keep in step with the Spirit. (NIV)

Fruit is the outcome of servant-heartedness. Serving is not about fulfilling a role or accomplishing duties; it is about living life rooted in Jesus' love, following his example of servant-heartedness and seeing him bring forth fruit in your life. It's a process of walking and working with Jesus, getting to know him and seeing him transform and work through you.

I help every year at a children's summer camp. One year, our teaching programme focused on the fruit of the Spirit. Each day we talked about a different quality of this fruit, thinking up real-life examples of how God's fruit can show itself in our lives. For kindness, we talked about sharing what we have with our friends – and even those who aren't our friends. For gentleness, we talked about listening well. For self-control, we discussed how we can manage anger and show understanding.

With each quality of the Spirit's fruit, we saw that it was about looking outwards: looking to other people and seeing how we can best serve them. All of it, we found, is rooted in love, that first quality listed in Galatians 5.

Reflect on your own life: what fruit has God brought as you have followed him? Think back one year, five years, 30 years: how are you different now to how you were then? How have you grown and changed into a person whose life shows the fruit of the Spirit? In what ways would you like to continue to grow?

Keep praying that the Spirit will challenge and encourage you to inhabit that space of servant-heartedness: that way of being yourself, rooted in his love, that leads to serving him. Look out for the fruit.

Father, thank you that as we grow in servant-heartedness, you bring forth fruit. Make me into a person who chooses to follow you day by day, keeping in step with your Spirit and seeing your life spring forth.

HANNAH FYTCHE

Fruit and fruitfulness

Chris Leonard writes:

Are you getting your five a day? Or is it ten now? Fruit and veg, that is, ideally as multicoloured and with as great a variety as possible. You know it makes sense for your health and well-being, lessening your chance of diabetes, heart problems, strokes, cancer and the like, all of which shorten lives and overstretch healthcare resources.

Have you considered not only eating but growing five, or more, a day? Not everyone has a garden or even space for an indoor plant-pot. We're fortunate enough to have both, but we'd still be hard-pressed to grow five different fruits every day of the year, although our freezer allows me to enjoy our summer crop of raspberries and blackcurrants with my daily breakfast cereal. Their intense taste zings dark midwinter mornings alive.

To have good fruit in our lives, though, we don't need freezers or gardens. The Bible urges us to grow the kind of fruit that is really good for our own well-being in body, mind and spirit. And others will benefit, too, from the fruit of our lives which will help establish the kind of all-round peace, wholeness, abundance and health that's summed up in the biblical Hebrew word 'shalom'. Such fruit is both a sign of and a growth mechanism for God's kingdom. He gives us the seed, water and nutrients and urges us to be fruitful. As fruit grows in our own lives, we become more like Jesus – more loving, patient, kind and so on. And like fruit-bearing plants we multiply, by giving others a taste and by spreading seeds.

Maybe we can learn, too, from bad fruit – poisonous or mouldy, perhaps – that leaves a nasty taste, a stomachache or worse. And from neglected fruit. One January, I saw an apple tree in someone's garden and beneath it a perfect circle of yellow, rotting apples whose waste saddened me. Could they not have been shared?

Fruit's abundance, its variety of colour, shape and taste – all speak of God's creativity and generosity. Though we can only scratch the surface over the next two weeks, fruit and fruitfulness make for a rich and juicy topic to explore together – and they appear right through the Bible, from Genesis to Revelation. So, let's begin… at the beginning!

Creation and multiplication

God created… trees bearing fruit with seed in it according to their kinds. And God saw that it was good… God blessed them and said to them, 'Be fruitful and increase in number.' (NIV)

If preachers mention fruit and fruitfulness, how do you feel? Sometimes I'll feel guilty, hearing whispers like these: 'You're not being fruitful enough. How many people have you led to the Lord? Not many. Too often your seed falls on the wrong bit of the field and dies. As for the fruits of the spirit – like joy, peace and, especially, patience – not always there as they should be, are they?'

It's so easy to feel misplaced guilt, to write ourselves off as failing to reach some impossible standards that we think God has set. Yet Hosea 14:8 says: 'Your fruitfulness comes from me.'

Genesis gives us a distinctive take on fruit and fruitfulness. Both are hardwired into God's design for creation. The whole ecosystem he made is not only sustainable but also involves multiplication among plant species and the animal kingdom. The very first commandment that God gave people was 'be fruitful and increase in number; fill the earth'. The human race has certainly accomplished that – even overdone it! So what was Eden's forbidden fruit? Not sexual knowledge, as some have inferred. No, if God told people to reproduce, sex must be among what he pronounced 'very good'. (Like everything else he created, it can be abused if we fail to follow his plans for delight and growth within committed relationships of self-giving love and trust.) No, *rebellion* was the forbidden fruit. Putting ourselves, not him, in charge: that poisons everything.

As we explore fruitfulness further, keep remembering that God has hardwired it into creation – and has promised spiritual fruitfulness for us who follow him. We're not perfect, but fruit will grow if we trust and stay close to him.

Thank you, Lord, for your good gift of fruitfulness lavished on all creation from the beginning – and now on your new creations like us. Thank you that any and all of our good fruitfulness comes from you.

CHRIS LEONARD

Abundant provision – enjoy, grow, feed

He waters the mountains… The land is satisfied by the fruit of his work. He makes grass grow for the cattle, and plants for people to cultivate – bringing forth food from the earth: wine that gladdens human hearts, oil to make their faces shine, and bread that sustains their hearts. (NIV)

Consider the richness and abundance of God's creation, then focus on all the different fruits he made for people and animals to enjoy – their different colours, textures and tastes. What's your favourite? There are so many that I love. Some, sour or bitter, tingle my taste buds when mixed with other foodstuffs. Some are essential for health – remember sailors developing scurvy on long voyages, then discovering the efficacy of oranges and lemons? Think of the pleasures and necessities fruit provides. Grapes make wine. Oil from olives not only made people's faces shine but powered lamps in the days before electric lights. Even the fruit of deadly nightshade – belladonna – once made into drugs, can regulate heart rate or help people with Parkinson's disease. As we read yesterday, 'I give you every seed-bearing plant on the face of the whole earth and every tree that has fruit with seed in it. They will be yours for food' (Genesis 1:29).

I'm sure God takes pleasure in people discovering surprising uses for fruit, or cultivating new varieties. I imagine he greatly approves the soft fruits and apples I grow in our garden – and often he'll use them to communicate with me as I tend and pick them. Take the raspberries hiding beneath leaves which can only be seen from certain angles. Having moved right along the row, I'm convinced I've picked all the ripe ones, yet, approaching from a different direction, bending down, moving the branches around and leaning right into the middle of the canes, I spot as many more again. Our raspberries are not only delicious; they've also become living parables, teaching me to look out for different perspectives and angles on specific situations.

Thank you, Lord, for fruits – for the nourishment, health and enjoyment they give us, for their amazing tastes, properties and variety, for the ability to cultivate them and for all they show to us of you.

CHRIS LEONARD

First fruits

Bring the best of the first fruits of your soil to the house of the Lord your God. (NIV)

These days, all manner of fruit is available to buy at any season, but it's very special to plant, tend and wait, then pick and taste the first fruits of something you have grown. Giving such fruit to God suggests giving of our best – that which we're most thrilled about. It signifies thankfulness, too, and an acknowledgement that all our fruitfulness comes from him. Perhaps there's a 'loaves and fishes' principle, too: give the little you have this moment and God's generosity will keep providing plenty for all.

Crops, including fruit, are there for us to eat and enjoy, but also to give away – recipients in this passage include needy people and wild animals as well as the Lord. The book of Exodus specifies how the ancient Israelites were to make these sacrificial gifts, but today what do we leave for, or give to, the poor? Maybe we donate money to charities, or our time and expertise to people in need. Or could it be we are so anxious for a bargain, or to pay less for wages or services, that nothing is left for those living on or below the poverty line? What about animal life? My daughter's infant school assemblies sang endlessly about feeding birds in wintertime. Many people do that, but sacrifices in today's society might include also leaving space for wildlife whose habitat is often under huge pressure, or spending extra time and money seeking goods and packaging that are the least harmful to the natural environment.

And then first fruits. Our church might not know what to do with our first raspberries or apples if we brought them to church, though I'm sure many people in our community would appreciate them. And though fresh produce poses logistical problems for the food banks that have become life-savers for many, supermarkets often have collection points for donating the longer-lasting purchases that keep food banks supplied.

Lord, whether or not we grow food, keep us mindful of the attitudes you want us to cultivate and show us how we can best give to help those in need, to help the planet and to gladden your heart.

CHRIS LEONARD

Not all fruit is good

'You are free to eat from any tree in the garden; but you must not eat from the tree of the knowledge of good and evil, for when you eat from it you will certainly die.' (NIV)

Have you ever poisoned anyone? I have. In the early days of our marriage, I poisoned my husband – and myself. I'd soaked dried kidney beans overnight as instructed but, by the time I'd returned from work to cook our evening meal, I had no recollection of the packet's warning about the time needed to boil them. Ours tasted fine, if a little crunchy, but we were both up all night, surviving because of our bodies' ability to expel the poison through much vomiting. It was so memorably horrible that I've used tinned kidney beans ever since!

God knows that not all fruit, real or metaphorical, is good for us. His commands are made not to restrict unreasonably and make us miserable, but for our benefit – as in, 'The Sabbath was made for man, not man for the Sabbath' (Mark 2:27). God knows we need some rest – or we'll work ourselves, and any we employ, to death. There again, our marriage has survived more than 40 years since that (unintentional) poisoning, in part because we have heeded God's commands about not committing adultery or coveting our neighbours' spouses.

Adam and Eve didn't take heed of the one thing God told them not to do, nor of his warning that certain death would result from their disobedience. All the good, luscious fruit were no longer theirs for the picking once God banished them from Eden. He told the man, 'Cursed is the ground because of you; through painful toil you will eat food from it all the days of your life. It will produce thorns and thistles for you, and you will eat the plants of the field' (Genesis 3:17–18).

Who would choose mistrust and rebellion over loving friendship with their creator? Hang on – not listening to and trusting him, going my own way – I do that! Thank the Lord for the cross, his antidote for our self-poisoning.

CHRIS LEONARD

Spoilt fruit

The Lord called you a thriving olive tree with fruit beautiful in form. But with the roar of a mighty storm he will set it on fire, and its branches will be broken. (NIV)

So many things can spoil fruit. What we grow hasn't been affected by fire or storm (yet), but, one year, codling moths devastated our apple crop. Beetles will hatch their grubs in our raspberries if I don't keep careful watch and, until we relocated their canes inside a fruit cage, clumsy pigeons used to break them down. I'm upset by such things, just as I was to see that perfect circle of apples rotting all round a stranger's tree – such neglect and waste of good gifts.

When I read Jeremiah 2:7, I feel God's pain – 'I brought you into a fertile land to eat its fruit and rich produce. But you came and defiled my land and made my inheritance detestable.' He had tended, rescued and nurtured these people. He had forgiven them so many times, but the only chance of their responding to him now was after experiencing his destructive power. His hope, as he sent them into the shame, isolation and powerlessness of exile, was that they would return to him.

I guess it's a bit like this: if we had an invasion of honey fungus, one way forward would be to destroy most of our plants, thus depriving the fungus of food for a few years. Then, after we'd disinfected the soil, we could try replanting.

Do the ever-more destructive storms and fires being experienced around the world mean that the human race is not responding to prophetic warnings over the damage that our collective greed has wrought? Are they a natural result of human-caused pollution and burning of hydrocarbons bringing the predicted disasters of climate change? Natural justice, you might say. Save us, Lord!

Lord, teach us how to nurture rather than destroy the planet on which we live. Forgive us. Help us to nurture rather than destroy one another as well.

CHRIS LEONARD

Fruit restored

The Lord's justice will dwell in the desert, his righteousness live in the fertile field. The fruit of that righteousness will be peace; its effect will be quietness and confidence forever… Though hail flattens the forest and the city is levelled completely, how blessed you will be, sowing your seed by every stream. (NIV)

According to the Bible, the fruitfulness of the land itself depends on people's spiritual fruit – their righteousness and trust in God. That makes natural sense when you think what terrible effects the opposite has on land and on crops. War and enforced people-movements cause ruin and famine. By contrast, what a beautiful picture Isaiah gives here of a people on whom 'the Spirit is poured from on high'.

God's gracious promises that Isaiah recorded were never fully realised: this was because, after their return from exile, God's 'chosen people' did not follow his ways. Those who had been left behind to care for the land came from the poorer end of society. When the wealthier, more powerful and educated exiles returned, most looked on those who had remained as inferior beings, evicting them from the land they had been caring for. When foreign superpowers imposed heavy taxes, the returnees extracted the payments from the already-destitute remnant. Justice being abandoned led to consequences: quietness and confidence were conspicuous by their absence, along with free-ranging cattle and any certainty that seed sown would ever flourish.

God loves to bless and to rescue, but if we jump straight back into the mess from which he's rescued us, what is he to do? He's allowed us to make choices, but he won't save us every time from the consequences of making bad ones. When Israel kept refusing to tend the splendid 'vineyard' in which he had placed them, when all his love and care produced only rotten fruit, he took the ultimate step of sending his Son, who died to rescue us all.

Let the parable of the tenants in the vineyard, as told in Matthew 21:33–43, speak to you.

CHRIS LEONARD

What kind of fruit are you?

The righteous will flourish like a palm tree... grow like a cedar of Lebanon... flourish in the courts of our God... still bear fruit in old age... stay fresh and green, proclaiming, 'The Lord is upright; he is my Rock, and there is no wickedness in him.' (NIV)

Compare this with Psalm 1:1–3 – 'Blessed is the one who does not walk in step with the wicked or stand in the way that sinners take or sit in the company of mockers, but whose delight is in the law of the Lord, and who meditates on his law day and night. That person is like a tree planted by streams of water, which yields its fruit in season and whose leaf does not wither – whatever they do prospers.'

Years ago, I bought a small citrus plant in a pot. Since then, it has trebled in size and flowers sweetly every year, but only after the hot summer of 2018 did it bear fruit. Looking like miniature oranges, they're extremely bitter, but we found delicious and unusual Filipino recipes that use them to marinade meat and fish. Enjoy the thought that God may be planning to use your gifts, your 'fruit', in unusual ways in the days to come, perhaps quite differently from the way he is using them now.

What kind of 'tree' are you? Big or small? Trees start small but how they grow if rooted in a safe environment and supplied with enough moisture and nutrients. Cedars of Lebanon are famously magnificent, but size isn't everything. Our first apple tree, grown on dwarfing rootstock, produces boxes full of apples every year. Another tasty variety yields well only every other year. It's good to know that our spiritual 'fruit', too, appears at the appointed season, when the tree has the right conditions *and* enough maturity. It's unlikely to be visible all the time.

We'll be looking more tomorrow at what Jesus had to say about growing fruit. Meanwhile, read these two psalms again and talk with the Lord about them. Perhaps because I'm reaching state pension age, he's been encouraging me that I can still bear fruit and stay fresh and green into old age, without withering.

Thank you, Lord, for the way you speak to us through your creation and through the Bible. May we learn to grow willingly, in the way you designed, letting you nourish us.

CHRIS LEONARD

Bear fruit

'You did not choose me, but I chose you and appointed you so that you might go and bear fruit – fruit that will last – and so that whatever you ask in my name the Father will give you. This is my command: love each other.' (NIV)

It is all so very simple. The Father loves the Son, who loves us. All we really have to do is to keep accepting his love, fully, all the time, choosing to live from that place of being loved by him, letting his love flow through us back to God and out to other people. Of course, when we know he loves us and when we love him, we'll do what he wants. We'll ask only for what he loves to give, rather than anything that might work against his love. He will continue to be generous, empowering us with his very life so that we can't help but bear fruit that will last.

So simple, and yet so difficult. Knowing I'm loved that much by all-powerful and yet gentle Jesus, what stops me trusting him, even over little matters? Why do I grow my fears instead of confidence in him, a siege mentality instead of a loving openness towards him and others? What makes me think that I've got to work it all out myself, resulting in the rotten fruits of stress, worry, exhaustion and irritability? What makes me surmise that, if I do everything right, he will love me more? Why risk poisonous fruits such as self-righteousness, religiosity and judging others?

I am vulnerable – we all are. We've all been hurt in life – let down by others, betrayed, rejected and loved only incompletely. But if we made ourselves fully vulnerable to his love, letting him love through us, what fruits of healing and restoration might grow and multiply? Let's take time to speak to Jesus and then to our own souls, as often the psalmists did, declaring: 'Jesus' life and love can flow through me.' Then just let him do it!

Lord, you've chosen and appointed me! You demonstrated your love by dying in agony for me, your power by rising to live again so your life and love can flow through me. Once more, I surrender.

CHRIS LEONARD

Pruning

'I am the true vine, and my Father is the gardener. He cuts off every branch in me that bears no fruit, while every branch that does bear fruit he prunes so that it will be even more fruitful.' (NIV)

After the encouraging picture of Jesus' love and life flowing through us to produce fruit, here we find harsher words. Pruning to produce more fruit I understand. How vines grow! Our two grape vines would strangle our home like Sleeping Beauty's castle unless we hacked away at them regularly. I know commercial vines are kept tiny to make larger, juicier fruit. I know, too, that we Christians need spiritual 'pruning' from time to time.

But human branches being cut off for lack of fruit, then 'thrown into the fire and burned', has overtones of the Spanish Inquisition that are surely not intended – Jesus' forgiveness and restoration come before his condemnation. Many of us go through dry, fruitless times, or feel unconnected with God for a season, yet even if we ourselves were the cause of the alienation, his gentle persistence will most often 'reattach' and make us fruitful again.

So was Jesus speaking of 'you-plural' branches? The only outward sign that living 'Jesus-branches' once flourished in a locality may be some church architecture converted into living, shopping or entertainment space. What happened? Did the former congregation die out because they failed to spread the gospel seed? Or might bad fruit – bad attitudes that interrupt the flow of Jesus' life – have poisoned the church? One church near where we once lived kept themselves to themselves, never associating with other Christians; it's now defunct. We know of another that fixed their focus less on Jesus and caring for one another, and more on hype. Leadership quarrels followed and many formerly faithful and fruitful disciples suffered lasting damage. Others dispersed and, as in the early church, began new works as part of fully attached 'branches' in a different area of the 'vine', where they continue to bear much fruit.

Lord, you'll say different things to different people through the difficult bits of this passage, but we can all pray: keep us intimately attached to you and to other disciples, so your life can flow out through us.

CHRIS LEONARD

Dying to be fruitful

'Very truly I tell you, unless a grain of wheat falls to the ground and dies, it remains only a single seed. But if it dies, it produces many seeds.' (NIV)

I love to visit 'Kew in the Country', whose Millennium Seed Bank conserves all of Britain's and 25% of the world's plant species as seeds, stored underground in controlled conditions. Seeds are both extraordinary time capsules and potent symbols of the principle of resurrection that God designed into his creation. Tiny and apparently lifeless in the soil, until temperature, moisture or even fire releases them to life and growth, they resurrect, not as seed at first, but as seed-forming plants. God's way is often to start small without apparent power or show – think baby, think acorn. Then think all that might come from one oak tree or one Christian and supremely from Jesus – all this growing, supporting and reproducing, way into the future.

Dying, being lifted up on a cross in order to 'draw all people to himself' – it's extraordinary! Jesus healed, rescued, taught, helped the poor, worked miracles – yet it took his death, burial and resurrection for the seed of the gospel to sprout, grow and then spread all over the world. So many Christians since have literally lost their lives that others might gain Jesus' eternal life. We owe them, as well as him, thanks.

But how does all this apply to us who aren't being called literally to die for him? Well, another thing I've noticed, and experienced, is how God sometimes gives us a dream or a vision – and then nothing happens for years. Despite all our efforts, it lies dead and buried. We question what it was all about; then, just as we've almost forgotten about it, suddenly it springs to life and exponential growth. That process makes us rely on God rather than imagining we could have done it by ourselves. He wastes nothing; but brings all good to fruition.

A thought: if John 12:25 (about hating your life) worries you, think on Philippians 1:21: 'To live is Christ and to die is gain.'

CHRIS LEONARD

What kind of fruit?

'By their fruit you will recognise them. Do people pick grapes from thorn-bushes, or figs from thistles? Likewise, every good tree bears good fruit, but a bad tree bears bad fruit. A good tree cannot bear bad fruit, and a bad tree cannot bear good fruit.' (NIV)

Jesus was warning here about false prophets, 'wolves in sheep's clothing', who could decimate his flock. How were his disciples to tell them apart from God's true servants? By what they did and how they lived. Jesus goes on to say the same about all who profess to follow him. If we hear the truth but don't live by it, if we call him Lord but don't do as he commands, we too will bear bad fruit – a sobering thought.

What then is good fruit? Ephesians 5:9 says 'all goodness, righteousness and truth', and Galatians 5:22–23 lists 'love, joy, peace, forbearance, kindness, goodness, faithfulness, gentleness and self-control'. Fruit here seems to be less about multiplication – going and making disciples of Jesus – than about each growing to be more like Jesus.

If you plant a seed – say, an apple pip – any resultant plant won't produce apples for several years. Gardening books insist that discarding the first year's fruits makes young trees stronger and more productive, long-term. Of course, God works mightily through very new Christians sometimes, and can make violent people gentle overnight. But normally he gives us room to grow, time to change, to absorb his love for us and thus grow to be more loving and fruitful.

It's clearly important that our leaders and prophets grow good fruit in their lives, rather than strive for personal kudos or gain. But they are not Jesus – we can't expect them to be perfect. Even the most saintly people have flaws on which the Holy Spirit is still working. That's got me thinking again about 'branches'. If flaws and rotten fruit are not to multiply, we all, especially our 'branch' leaders and those with prophetic vision, need to be accountable to and pray for one another.

Lord, when we persist in bad attitudes and produce bad fruit, alert us. Help us to apologise and put right any damage we have done. Grow your goodness in us. Encourage us to pray for our leaders, too.

CHRIS LEONARD

Results – gospel spreads

The gospel is bearing fruit and growing throughout the whole world – just as it has been doing among you since the day you heard it and truly understood God's grace. (NIV)

Paul's ministry was certainly fruitful. He both seeded and nurtured faith within the new believers. Back then, it was all so new! For example, Paul, having been forced to flee after a very short time in Thessalonica, worried about how the tiny band of new believers might survive. He dispatched Timothy, who reported back that, despite no further missionary input, the new Christians in Thessalonica had become renowned in all Macedonia and Achaia for their changed lives and faith in God. They evangelised and even endured persecution with joy. Read 1 Thessalonians 1 for yourself; it's probably Paul's earliest surviving letter, and he's thrilled to discover that this gospel really does work. Its fruit will reproduce itself, true to type, throughout the world.

My faith in the transforming power of this gospel has been reinvigorated lately, too, in a women's prison of all places. The gospel 'seeds' weren't sown by me. But I saw good fruit growing in changed lives and real joy filling women in far from easy circumstances. It moved and encouraged me that those with learning difficulties, or lacking any education, often showed the most profound knowledge of him. Many were tested when it came to forgiving others – but as God helped these women to forgive, they rejoiced in feeling so much lighter. Though I'm sure they all have bad days, I saw predominantly honesty, thankfulness, faith, love and hope shining there. I've rarely been with a group of people more focused on Jesus; he is truly their all in all, their lifeline. As Paul said in 1 Corinthians 3:6 – whoever planted or watered the seed, 'God has been making it grow.' Only he has that power!

Use Paul's great prayer in Colossians 1:9–12 to help you pray for yourself and for any new or struggling Christians that you know. Thank the Lord for the fruits you see.

CHRIS LEONARD

Results – first fruits mature

We ourselves, who have the first fruits of the Spirit, groan inwardly as we wait eagerly for our adoption to sonship, the redemption of our bodies. (NIV)

The word 'firstfruits' appears often in the Old Testament, referring to gifts that people offered to God. Paul turns this around, saying God gives us 'the firstfruits of the Spirit'. Thrice elsewhere in his letters, Paul declares that God gives us his Holy Spirit as a 'deposit', guaranteeing what is to come. 1 Corinthians 15:20 proclaims Christ as the first fruits of those who die and are made alive – if Christ rose, so will we. In James 1:18, we ourselves are 'a kind of firstfruits of all he created', since the Father 'chose to give us birth through the word of truth'.

How exciting that all of these passages look forward to God making everything even better than his original plans in creating the world! C.S. Lewis used the analogy of 'shadowlands' to express that, in this life, we see only a pale shadow of the glories to come.

Imagine when we have the fully ripened, perfect fruits of the Spirit, when we've grown enough to appreciate and use them to the full, where nothing, not even we ourselves, can turn God's gifts sour and mouldy in our mouths, nothing can wither them with frost while still beyond our reach on the tree. Imagine being made fully alive in Christ, who came to give us life in all its fullness. We've glimpsed a little of that, and a little of the Holy Spirit, already. Hopefully we're growing into more – whether that happens through suffering, through love and kindness or through wonder, questioning, trust. Meanwhile our beautiful, flawed world is waiting and groaning until we come into our own full inheritance as God's children within the new earth that God will create.

Lord, we want more: more of you – of your love, ways and closeness, of your melody and harmonies. We long for all your creation to fulfil its truest perfection; we long to be part of that, through knowing you.

CHRIS LEONARD

Eden restored – and more!

On each side of the river stood the tree of life, bearing twelve crops of fruit, yielding its fruit every month. And the leaves of the tree are for the healing of the nations. (NIV)

At first, Eden was perfect, though a little bit underpopulated. Then humanity rebelled, embracing evil. Creation was polluted, stopped from working as perfectly as God had intended. But where are we heading now? Well, the picture given in Revelation replaces Genesis' beautiful empty garden with a new earth, within which is a fair and gracious city. A river whose water is life flows from God's throne and along its main thoroughfare, and trees line its banks. Being so well-watered, those trees always bear fruit, so there's plenty for the multitudes to enjoy.

The city is like none we know. Its gates are always open, welcoming everyone inside to share in God's goodness and provision. With the leaves of the trees being 'for the healing of the nations', there's no conflict and, with the ever-fruiting trees, no competition for food. With God in charge and Jesus as our light, fear and defensiveness are redundant, evil banished. Only the love of God remains, in which all share, worshipping him. Relationships will be deep and community true there. Each will bring our unique gifts of creativity, skills, songs and ways of expressing love to add to the colour, harmony and joy.

So that's it, folks. That's where all this fruitfulness and seed-sowing is heading. That's what I believe, anyway. It sounds a lot more plausible and worthwhile than hanging about on clouds playing harps – more like what God would dream up, too. Having said that, no words, not even those in Revelation, can give more than a washed-out hint of a blotched outline of the fullness of life and the depth of loving community that we'll experience there. Best of all, of course, we'll be with him!

Lord God, thank you again that all fruitfulness, in every sense, comes from you. Encourage us with your hope, fill us with your love and may all the fruit we bear be fruit for your kingdom.

CHRIS LEONARD

Peter's letters

Lyndall Bywater writes:

Being an early adopter isn't always easy. When I was young, my parents began buying a new range of cleaning products. The company used a direct sales method, so instead of buying from a shop, you'd buy from a friend or acquaintance who'd signed up to be a salesperson for the company. The products in question impressed my parents greatly, and I remember them telling me that the all-purpose cleaner could 'get stains out of pretty much anything'.

Fast-forward a while and you'll find me at boarding school, having just spilt something down my clean dress. In my keenness to get the stain out as quickly as possible, I went to ask a member of staff if she had any of this wonder-working stain-remover. She had no idea what I was talking about. I was frustrated. Not only was my dress doomed, but this poor woman was missing out on something utterly magical in her life.

It probably won't surprise you to hear that I haven't seen a bottle of that cleaner for decades, but I can still remember the zeal of thinking we'd discovered something that was going to take the world by storm. Peter wrote to another group of people who were early adopters, not of cleaning products but of a faith story which truly was life-changing. The Bible contains two of his letters, written to little communities of Jesus-followers dotted across Asia Minor. Peter had been with Jesus throughout his three-year ministry. He had been in Jerusalem during that fateful Passover when his master had gone to the cross. He had seen the empty tomb and the risen Christ. Now, as one of the church's first leaders, it was his job to understand this new Christian faith and to teach it wherever he went. There were all sorts of versions of it springing up around the region, and Peter knew that he had been given a special trust: to strengthen the early adopters and help them live out this newly revealed truth.

Two millennia later, you and I can't really call ourselves 'early adopters', but we still have times when we feel out on a limb, like we don't fit in or people don't quite get us. Peter has life-giving words for anyone who feels that way. If that's you, I hope reading his letters will encourage you.

Scattered

From Peter, an apostle of Jesus the Anointed One, to the chosen ones who have been scattered abroad like 'seed' into the nations living as refugees... *You are not forgotten*, **for you have been chosen and destined by Father God. (TPT)**

There is a story that Sylvester Stallone was once so poor that he had to sell his dog for $25. He called it the lowest point of his life. Not long afterwards, he started making the immensely successful *Rocky* films, and the rest is history. If you were concerned about the dog, you'll be heartened to know that he bought it back with his first pay cheque... for $15,000.

Sometimes we really do hit rock bottom. Peter was writing to Christians who had had to flee because of violent persecution. They had had to leave homes, families and church communities, ending up as refugees, scattered throughout the surrounding nations. So what did he say? What could he say, to help them make sense of such traumatic events?

Peter's very first words were designed to help his readers see their circumstances from a different perspective. They may have ended up in places they didn't want to be, but it wasn't because God had abandoned them or forgotten them. If they'd been scattered, then it was in the way a farmer scatters seed. Having been with Jesus, the image of seed being scattered and bearing fruit would have been very familiar to Peter (see Mark 4:1–20). And now he could see the master gardener's handiwork, as those persecuted Christians took the good news of Jesus to places it had never been before.

Peter wanted his readers to know that they'd been planted by a wise and gentle hand, and I imagine he'd want us to know that, too. Even if you feel like you've been dumped somewhere you never wanted to be, take heart. God himself, the master gardener, has placed you where you are, and he'll pour out his love and grace on you so that you can bear fruit, even there.

Father God, I may never write a blockbuster movie, but I do believe that you have good things in store for me. Thank you for what you're going to do in this place where you've planted me.

LYNDALL BYWATER

Privileged

**Your life is a journey you must travel with a deep consciousness of God.
It cost God plenty to get you out of that dead-end, empty-headed life
you grew up in. He paid with Christ's sacred blood, you know. (MSG)**

Was there a food you hated as a child? Did the adults around you insist on
telling you that you should be grateful for it, because the children in Africa
don't have such lovely things? And did you mutter under your breath
that they should just go ahead and put it in the post to Africa? It's hard to
teach children gratitude, because they simply don't yet understand the
value of what they've been given.

In a rather more theological way, Peter was having that same conversation with his readers. He knew they were reeling from all that had
happened to them and didn't like where they'd ended up, but he wanted
them to understand what they did have, so they could practise gratitude.
They had revelation: they'd heard the whole story of Jesus' death and
resurrection – something the prophets only ever got hints of. They'd been
restored: lifted out of death and filled with boundless life – something not
even angels got to experience. And they'd been ransomed: set free from
the stranglehold of sin because God paid a price for them – not with gold
or silver, but with his very own lifeblood.

When you've been on the road a while, the wonderful things God has
done for you can start to feel over-familiar. Why not revisit the three Rs:

- **Revelation**: Is there a truth about God of which you have become
  more sure over the past year?
- **Restoration**: Are there things which have come alive in you recently –
  things which used to seem dead and hopeless?
- **Ransom**: Are there habits or tendencies with which you've been living,
  even though you know the price has been paid to set you free?

---

*Lord Jesus, thank you for spending your lifeblood so that I can be free.
Father God, thank you for restoring me and giving me life. Holy Spirit, thank
you for revealing the beauty of God to me.*

LYNDALL BYWATER

You're a brick

As you come to him, a living stone rejected by [humankind] but in the sight of God chosen and precious, you yourselves like living stones are being built up as a spiritual house, to be a holy priesthood, to offer spiritual sacrifices acceptable to God through Jesus Christ. (ESV)

On 15 April 2019, we watched as the cathedral of Notre Dame in Paris nearly burned down. What I will always remember most clearly, though, was not the fire but the crowds of people gathered in the streets throughout the night, pouring out their hearts in prayer and singing, desperate to know whether that magnificent building would be saved.

Persecuted and scattered to far-off places, many of Peter's readers had already lived through some very tough times, but there was even more to their suffering than that. Just a few decades after Jesus' death and resurrection, the temple in Jerusalem had been destroyed. Disasters like the fire at Notre Dame give us a glimpse into how precious a building can be to those who have worshipped there, but nothing in our own time can adequately convey how important the temple was to Jewish people. Many of Peter's readers would have been Jewish believers, and they would have felt bewildered and bereft at the loss of this physical structure which had been God's chosen dwelling-place on earth.

When I read about Peter in the gospels, he strikes me as a practical chap, and his approach here is no different. The temple's gone, he seems to be saying, but don't lose sleep over that. God is building a new temple, and it's you lot! They may have felt lost, scattered and hopeless, but God had a whole new plan which put them right back in the heart of the action. There would be a temple right where they found themselves, and it would be made of them.

Have you been feeling out on a limb lately? You're a vital brick in God's hands. He is building something in the place where you find yourself, and it includes you.

LYNDALL BYWATER

Valuing people

Recognise the value of every person and continually show love to every believer. Live your lives with great reverence and in holy awe of God. Honour your rulers. (TPT)

Let me ask you a challenging question: when you feel insecure, how does that affect the way you treat others? I have to confess this can be a struggle for me at times. Being blind, I regularly feel 'othered' – aware that people are treating me as different or less able – and in my pain, I often respond by being ungracious. Isn't it only fair to treat others the way they treat me?

Some of the Christians Peter was writing to had developed a reputation for being on the ungracious side of feisty. Frustrated by their marginalisation and poor treatment by the authorities, they had started to become aggressively obstructive, reasoning that they should fight fire with fire, to protect themselves in the midst of a hostile society. That's perhaps why Peter returned again and again to this idea of living good, upright lives in the sight of everyone. Our human way is often to conclude that if people can't respect us, then why should we respect them? But Peter had been around Jesus, a man who treated every individual he encountered with honour, whether high-born or low, whether for him or against him.

Does that mean being a doormat? No! Being gracious doesn't mean we don't confront wrongdoing, and we may need to set boundaries that keep us safe from those who would harm us. But when we remember that each person is precious in God's eyes, then we can treat them graciously, even from within those boundaries.

One thing's for sure, though: it is hard to recognise the value of others when you don't believe you yourself have value. So next time you feel tempted to be ungracious towards somebody, stop and remember how precious you are in God's sight. It'll help you treat them the same way.

Father God, help me today to recognise the intrinsic value in every person I meet and to treat them with respect and dignity, no matter how I feel about them or how they are treating me.

LYNDALL BYWATER

Disagreeing well

Summing up: Be agreeable, be sympathetic, be loving, be compassionate, be humble. That goes for all of you, no exceptions. No retaliation. No sharp-tongued sarcasm. Instead, bless – that's your job, to bless. You'll be a blessing and also get a blessing. (MSG)

The last few years have taught me so much about how to disagree well. On a number of political and theological issues, I've found myself at the opposite end of the opinion spectrum to friends who I dearly love and trust, and since I seem to have friends who are pretty passionate about things, it has sometimes felt like those relationships have been stretched to breaking point. However, the one thing I've learnt above everything else is that deep, committed, releasing love is the ingredient which the world most admires. My friends who don't know Jesus have often been shocked by the way in which my Christian friends and I have actually grown closer as a result of our disagreements.

Yesterday, we got a taste of Peter's concern for the way his readers were behaving towards those around them, particularly those in authority. Today, we get a glimpse into how he wanted them to behave as a Christian family: how their marriages, churches and friendships should look. Like me and my friends, they probably disagreed about all sorts of things. Christianity has always transcended culture. There were very few hard-and-fast rules about things like what to wear or what to eat, so there would have been plenty of room for strong opinions and sharp differences.

Some translations do include 'like-minded' in verse 8, but since Peter often disagreed with his fellow apostles, we can assume he didn't mean his readers had to agree about everything. What he wanted was for them to prioritise love, humility and compassion. They didn't have to think alike, but they did have to match one another in their determination to put relationship above the desperate need to be right. Only then would the world know whose disciples they were (John 13:34–35).

Have you been putting too much emphasis on being right and not enough on loving? Stop for a moment and ask God to help you recalibrate. Choose today to see the person rather than their opinion.

LYNDALL BYWATER

Nothing and nowhere is beyond him

Jesus has the last word on everything and everyone, from angels to armies. He's standing right alongside God, and what he says goes. (MSG)

I heard a lovely story the other day. A priest was talking to some children about Easter and he asked if they had any idea why Jesus might have visited hell on Easter Saturday. One boy thought for a moment then said, 'Did he go looking for his friend, Judas?'

Today's passage is one of the most famous parts of Peter's letters. His reference to Jesus preaching to the spirits of the dead is known as the 'harrowing of hell', and it has been the subject of much debate over the centuries. What did Peter mean? Where did Jesus go exactly? Who did he preach to and what did he say? And why does Peter mention it? The theories are too many and too complex to do justice to them here, but neither did I want to skip over these verses for just being too mysterious.

I have no idea whether the boy in the story I heard was right, of course, but I do think his answer captures something of the essence of who Jesus is, and perhaps that's what Peter was trying to do for his readers. Perhaps they were in danger of getting bogged down by the strains and demands of living a Christian life in a hostile environment. Perhaps they were in danger of forgetting the absolute awesomeness of the one whose family they'd been baptised into. Perhaps they needed reminding that nothing is beyond him; that no one is buried so deep, lost so far away or imprisoned so hopelessly that they can't be rescued.

And perhaps you need reminding of that today too. Jesus didn't come to congratulate the righteous. He came to plunder hell (whether you take that as literal or metaphorical), to go to the darkest places, offering light, hope and freedom.

You probably know someone who's living their own kind of hell at the moment. As you pray for them, picture Jesus walking right into that terrible, dark place, taking their hand and leading them out into the light.

LYNDALL BYWATER

Making the difference

Since we are approaching the end of all things, be intentional, purposeful, and self-controlled so that you can be given to prayer. (TPT)

About 30 years ago, we started understanding that aerosols weren't good for the ozone layer. About 20 years ago, we started understanding more about the importance of recycling. About 10 years ago, we started shrinking our 'carbon footprint'. At each turn, I've felt powerless, wondering how these tiny changes can ever reverse the trend of climate change, but today I read that, for the first time in over 135 years, Britain has just gone a whole week without burning coal. Maybe those tiny choices did help after all.

When you feel small, insignificant and on the edge, it's hard to believe that your choices can change things. Peter's readers were living as tiny minorities in places where the moral culture probably seemed unchangeable. All sorts of ungodly practices were rife, and perhaps it felt easier to join in than stand out. But Peter saw something different. He'd seen the impact Jesus and their little band of friends had made on the towns and villages where they lived, and that was even before the resurrection. What might be possible now, if Jesus' followers scattered all over the region were to live differently – to live the Jesus way?

What does 'different' look like for you? I find the three words in The Passion Translation of verse 7 very helpful. Why not use them as a starting point for your thinking and praying today?

- **Intentional**: What small change can I make, to work towards the changes I long to see in the world around me?
- **Purposeful**: What can I do to make more time and energy for the things that matter most in life?
- **Self-controlled**: What do I need to step away from because it stops me living the Jesus life?

Think and pray about those three questions. Big changes start with small choices, so think of three small, simple choices you can make today to become more intentional, more purposeful and more self-controlled.

LYNDALL BYWATER

Pain and planting

Dear friends, don't be surprised at the fiery trials you are going through… Instead, be very glad – for these trials make you partners with Christ in his suffering, so that you will have the wonderful joy of seeing his glory when it is revealed to all the world. (NLT)

Close to the 9/11 memorial in Manhattan stands a Callery pear tree. Unlike so much else, it survived that fateful day of terror when the Twin Towers were destroyed. It was rescued, restored to full health and then planted beside the memorial pools, close to where it had originally grown. Each year, three of its seedlings are sent to places around the world which have experienced disaster. And so, out of unimaginable horror, new life continues to spring.

One of the strongest themes in Peter's writing is that of suffering. It's one of the reasons I find his letters a difficult read, because he spends so much time encouraging his readers to view suffering as something worthwhile and something to be glad of, whereas I just find it agonising and pointless. How do you welcome being hurt or seeing others hurt? How do you count it worthwhile when loved ones go through painful situations or when life seems to keep throwing problems at you?

The Callery pear seedlings help me understand. Suffering is inevitable, Peter was saying. It happened to Jesus and it'll happen to us. That's a given. But what if we can see it differently? What if we can endure it with faith, trusting that we'll survive and grow through it and believing that God will take from us seedlings of hope which he will plant into the lives of others?

If suffering is an all-too present reality in your life today, take courage. You may not be enjoying it, but you can draw strength from knowing that it counts for something. Even from the most cruel, futile situations, God can bring forth resurrection and transformation. I think that's what Peter meant when he said we'd have the joy of seeing God's glory in the end.

Have you seen God plant seeds from your own suffering? Can you think of situations where you've been able to support someone else because of what you yourself have been through? Stop and give thanks for that opportunity.

LYNDALL BYWATER

Confident and cared-for

Give all your worries and cares to God, for he cares about you. Stay alert! Watch out for your great enemy, the devil. He prowls around like a roaring lion, looking for someone to devour. (NLT)

I once went on a spiritual warfare training weekend, and the speaker used a rather amusing image to begin his talk. It was a picture of several large Alsatian dogs, all looking rather fierce and all restrained by leashes, and right in the foreground, strolling nonchalantly across their path, was a cat. It had the calm demeanour of one who knows that, though its enemies may be vicious and dangerous, it has nothing to fear because they are restrained and limited.

Today's passage is another rendering of that same reassuring message. Verses 8 and 9 are one of the most famous passages in scripture when it comes to teaching on spiritual warfare. Peter's picture of the prowling lion is vivid and sobering. He had heard Jesus teach again and again on the reality of Satan, the enemy who seeks to oppose the work of God, and he wanted his readers to be alert to that reality. Yet the verses are all-too often taught in isolation. The picture of the lion belongs right next to the picture of the great shepherd, who loves us, lifts us up and longs to bear the weight of all our cares.

Talk of lions and shepherds would have had particular resonance for Peter and his Jewish readers. King David, that great shepherd-king, had protected his father's flock from attacks by all kinds of wild beasts, including lions. For Peter, wisdom was to recognise the danger of the lion, but faith was to know that the shepherd King is always stronger and on hand to protect us.

Does talk of the enemy leave you feeling anxious? If it does, remind yourself that you're not left to handle spiritual opposition alone. Your shepherd King has your back so you can walk with confidence.

LYNDALL BYWATER

A godly life

By his divine power, God has given us everything we need for living a godly life. We have received all of this by coming to know him, the one who called us to himself by means of his marvellous glory and excellence. (NLT)

When a seed falls from a tree, it already contains the raw material for a whole new tree: trunk and branches, roots and leaves. It may look insignificant, but it holds all the cells necessary to produce something huge and beautiful which may well stand for centuries, sheltering wildlife, producing fruit and weathering storms. And all from that tiny seed!

Seeds have featured several times during this series on Peter's letters, and we're back with them again today, because they're the best way to make sense of this astonishing truth in verse 3. I don't know about you, but I tend to view 'living a godly life' as something I'm not very good at. On my worst days I'd even say it's going to take a whole personality transplant! But that's not what Peter said. He said that that life of godliness is all already inside us, like an embryo, just waiting to grow. It got planted the moment we first said 'yes' to Jesus, and it's there now, growing within us by the power of the Holy Spirit. Godliness isn't a badge we earn by working really hard; it's not something that only comes when we get everything right. A godly life is already inside us; it just needs the right conditions to grow.

Once the seed is planted, the first thing a tree embryo does is to produce roots so it can access water. The second thing it does is to produce leaves so it can access sunlight. To me, the qualities listed in verses 5–7 look a lot like roots and leaves: things that keep us in the flow of God's Spirit. Even on your worst days, those qualities are growing in you. Your job is to keep nurturing them so they can grow even more.

Read through the list of qualities in verses 5–7. You may want to read them in several different versions to get a fresh perspective on the words. Which of those qualities do you need to nurture in yourself today?

LYNDALL BYWATER

Hold on tight

We did not follow cleverly devised stories *or* myths when we made known to you the power and coming of our Lord Jesus Christ, but we were eyewitnesses of his majesty [his grandeur, his authority, his sovereignty]. (AMP)

When I was a student, our university Christian Union experienced a particularly intense outpouring of the Holy Spirit. During those months, I had encounters with Jesus which still shape my Christian life even 25 years on: experiences which taught me, deepened me and brought me such joy. But there were people around who weren't sure if what was happening was 'of God', and I ended up in many tense debates about how we could be sure we didn't go astray. What I learnt through it all was that I could really only test my own heart, hold on to what I knew was God and trust the Holy Spirit to guide me.

Peter knew he was nearing the end of his days, and there's an urgent tension in his words. He knew what he'd lived with Jesus, with breathtaking moments like the transfiguration, and he knew those things had been foretold by the prophets of old – but now other so-called prophets had started to emerge who were questioning even the basic facts of Jesus' life. Perhaps they were saying that Peter was making things up or that he had had demonic experiences. What would happen when eyewitnesses to Jesus' life like him weren't alive anymore? How would the fledgling church stay strong and true? These questions clearly preoccupied Peter.

In the end, all he could do was to tell them to follow his own example: to read the scriptures (that's what he meant by 'the prophets'), and to hold on to what they had experienced of God. That combination of a head full of scripture and a heart full of lived experience of God through the Holy Spirit – that combination would be a light to them, even in the darkest times. And that combination is still the best light there is.

Reflect on one thing you really know about God: something you know in your head because you've read it in scripture, but something you also know in your heart because you've experienced it. Give thanks and hold it tight.

LYNDALL BYWATER

Let God do the judging

So you see, the Lord knows how to rescue godly people from their trials, even while keeping the wicked under punishment until the day of final judgement. (NLT)

If you're an avid reader of detective novels, like me, then you'll know that, when it comes to justice, patience is everything. If the wily crime-solver moves too soon, there won't be enough evidence to convict the perpetrator and they'll get off scot-free. Since those of us who read detective fiction tend to be the type who love seeing baddies get their comeuppance, this slow, methodical approach can be most frustrating, because we want the situation to be put to rights as soon as possible.

If yesterday's passage was Peter feeling anxious for the church after his death, then perhaps today's is his reassurance to himself. He had accepted that false prophets would come in, peddling their own agendas, but it wouldn't last forever. God would always have the last word.

It's easy to worry about people being wrong. We hear them say something we don't agree with or we get wind of them having done something we disapprove of, and it's as though our inner justice-seeker goes into overdrive. We worry about the people they might 'lead astray'. We want them stopped; we want someone to tell them how wrong they are. But that wasn't Peter's way. He didn't tell his readers to go on a crusade to weed out every false teacher and con artist. He simply reminded them of their history, of those stories of God dealing with wrongdoers in the fullness of his own good time.

I don't imagine Peter meant any of us to ignore wrongdoing. There is a right time to speak out and a right way to act justly, but ultimately his confidence lay in the truth that God himself is the one true and flawless judge, and he knows exactly when to step in and work justice.

Are you worrying about someone who's 'getting it wrong'? Why not hand them back to God? Let go of the need to set them straight. God sees and knows them. If he wants you to do anything, he'll guide you.

LYNDALL BYWATER

Church leadership gone bad

These people are dried-up riverbeds, waterless clouds pushed along by stormy winds – the deepest darkness of gloom has been prepared for them… They promise others freedom, yet they themselves are slaves to corruption, for people are slaves to whatever overcomes them. (TPT)

One of the greatest honours I've ever been given in life is to accompany women on their journey of healing from childhood sexual abuse. I'm not a professional, but some of my dearest friends have trusted me enough to tell me their stories, and it has been an amazing privilege to listen to them and to support them in whatever way I can. The stories are everything you'd imagine: harrowing, horrifying, heart-breaking and enraging. Nothing in life has ever made me so angry as those stories.

The Peter who wrote these epistles wasn't the impetuous young activist who walked with Jesus any more. For the most part, the tone of these letters is measured and gentle… until this passage. We will never know what experience prompted the writing of this tirade, but suddenly he was furious. Perhaps he had seen something of the trail of destruction which abusers leave behind them in the lives of those on whom they prey.

The thing that makes me saddest and most angry about the stories I've heard is how often abuse is perpetrated by those in church leadership, and that's exactly what Peter discovered almost 2,000 years ago. It's no consolation that there have always been Christian leaders who've done these things. But Peter knew a better day was coming, and so do I.

There will be a day when the vulnerable will be safe, when the wounded will be whole and when justice will be served on every act of cruelty, manipulation and violence ever committed. Until then, we keep going: we keep making safe spaces for people to tell their story, we help them to speak out if they want to, and we keep working to make sure we have healthy, trustworthy leaders in our churches.

To all of you who've suffered this kind of abuse: thank you for still choosing to walk the Christian life. You are precious to us, and your story challenges us to become more the church God wants us to be.

LYNDALL BYWATER

Two vital ingredients

Let the wonderful kindness and the understanding that come from our Lord and Saviour Jesus Christ help you to keep on growing. Praise Jesus now and forever! Amen. (CEV)

Let's finish this series with one last story about things that grow. I heard a Baptist minister telling of his visit to a Welsh coal mine and his astonishment on finding, amidst all the grime and coal dust, a perfectly white lily. He asked how the flower managed to stay so pure, and his tour guide answered that the lily's petals are so smooth that the black dust simply slides off.

How do we live in this broken, often grimy world of ours, yet still stay pure? How do we live the Jesus life when so much around us seems to pull in different directions? How do we blossom and bear fruit when we feel like outsiders? In his closing words, Peter summed up all his advice in two simple phrases: it's about receiving the gift of grace and seeking the treasure of understanding.

The Christian life is born in gift. God himself sought us out, planted us up, breathed life into us by his Spirit and gave us everything we need to live life his way. It's time to stop thinking you've got to prove yourself or earn his approval. You're his planting, tended and delighted in by the master gardener who loves you so very much.

But the Christian life is also a treasure trove you're invited to explore. None of it will be forced upon you, but if you're interested, there's an endless supply of resources available to help you live fruitfully, intentionally and creatively. However confusing and dark the world may seem, you can choose to be someone who understands where you've been planted and why he's put you there. You can tune into his heart, learn to live in the power of his Spirit and make a difference in the lives of those around you.

Father God, thank you for the gift of grace. Help me live as one who has received much. Thank you for the treasures I've yet to discover in your kingdom. Help me live as one who is hungry for more.

LYNDALL BYWATER

Some dos and don'ts from Jesus

Annie Willmot writes:

One of my son's favourite books is called *Hermie: A common caterpillar* by Max Lucado (Thomas Nelson, 2001). Hermie the caterpillar and his friend Wormie think they're common, and every night they ask God why they can't be like the other, more exciting creatures.

God's answer is always the same: that he's not yet finished with them and that he's making their hearts more like his.

That has become a prayer for our family. 'God, make our hearts more like yours.' And it's what I think about when I read Matthew 5—7.

Jesus' heart flows through the sermon on the mount. It's like he's flinging his arms open wide, welcoming us into his kingdom, sharing his heart for the world and inviting us to be more like him. The standards he sets are crazily high, but that's the point! We can't do it in our own power. It's an invitation into relationship with him and, because of God's grace, it's possible.

Imagine the scene: Jesus has travelled all over the place. He's possibly tired, maybe hungry, and he spots the crowds of people. He goes up a mountainside, sits down and begins to teach.

Nowadays, when we hear teaching, the preacher usually stands at the front of a room and we sit rather more formally in rows facing all in one direction ready to receive. In Jesus' day, it was customary for rabbis to teach sitting down and for everyone to gather around and sit at their feet. Remember that's what Mary did, when Jesus visited Lazarus, Mary and Martha; she knew it was important to get close and listen to him as he had something of great worth to share.

To me, there's something really inviting about that simple act of Jesus sitting with the crowds. I like to imagine myself sat at his feet, marvelling at the authority with which he spoke, already imagining how I will tell all my friends about how I got to hear Jesus.

Let's sit together at Jesus' feet as we listen to some of his sermon on the mountainside.

Don't lose flavour

'Let me tell you why you are here. You're here to be salt-seasoning that brings out the God-flavours of this earth. If you lose your saltiness, how will people taste godliness? You've lost your usefulness and will end up in the garbage.' (MSG)

I love salt. I have two kids under four, so I cook most of our meals without salt. Most days, I salt my food before I even try it, but sometimes I forget and I'm hit pretty quickly by the blandness.

Salt is powerful. It brings out flavour and can transform a meal. If it lost its saltiness, it would be pretty useless!

Jesus didn't mince words in his analogies. He makes it clear that God calls us to be flavoursome, sharing with others where we see him at work, bringing out 'the God-flavours'. And, if we don't, there really isn't any point to us!

How do we stay salty? How do we make sure that people see God in us?

Some days, I feel a bit bland. I might feel disconnected from God or disconnected from others around me. Often, I know that's through my own choice. However, I know that when I choose connection, those days are different. Connection with God, with people, with the world around me. When I connect with God, ask him to open my eyes to see him at work, and when I intentionally share that with people around me, I don't feel bland at all.

Without salt the food is still good for you, but adding salt takes it to a whole new level. We can do good things, we can be kind and generous, but when we do those things *and* share the richness of Christ in us we bring out those 'God-flavours'!

There's no use in a salt shaker just sitting on the table. We need to pick it up and shake it. If we want to stay salty, we need to choose to connect with God and let others see him at work in us.

God, help me to see you at work today and give me boldness to share what I see with others.

ANNIE WILLMOT

Do mean what you say

'All you need to say is simply "Yes," or "No"; anything beyond this comes from the evil one.' (NIV)

This passage is all about integrity. It was common in the culture at that time to talk big and make false oaths to impress. Jesus was making it clear that you didn't need to swear on oath but, instead, be honest.

Jesus was refreshingly honest. He said it like it was. Have you ever met people like that – not people who are rude but people whom you know you can always trust to mean what they say?

I used to find it really hard to say no. If I received an invitation somewhere, or if someone needed help, I always said yes. I was afraid of letting people down. The problem was that when it came to it, I was either so tired that I wasn't much help anyway or I let them down last-minute when I realised I didn't actually want to go!

I didn't think I was being dishonest, but the reality is that I wasn't showing integrity. I wasn't being open or vulnerable. I've worked hard to say what I mean, to let my 'Yes' be 'Yes' and my 'No' be 'No', and it has led to my having much deeper relationships.

My closest relationships are the ones with people who'll tell me they're exhausted and can't do something, rather than offer and then change their answer at the last minute. I've learned so much from those friendships.

Jesus' words are powerful – 'anything beyond this comes from the evil one' – but of course the devil doesn't want community or deep relationships! When we say what we mean, and honour each other and God with our words, our relationships are strengthened and we build intimacy and community.

What would today look like if you let your 'Yes' be 'Yes' and your 'No' be 'No'?
ANNIE WILLMOT

Do pray like this

'This is your Father you are dealing with, and he knows better than you what you need. With a God like this loving you, you can pray very simply.' (MSG)

I lead funerals, and often I will meet with a family who have said they want absolutely no religion, only to find when a slot for prayer or reflection is offered, they say, 'Well, of course we want the Lord's Prayer.'

Perhaps it's the familiarity of saying something they said at school or church when they were younger, or perhaps it's a sort of 'just-in-case' move at the end of a funeral. Whatever it is, I've found that many people want the comfort of praying it or hearing it prayed.

It's easy to dismiss the Lord's Prayer as being traditional or something we just say at church. I am often put off by things I view as traditional or liturgical. I can instantly dismiss them as not helpful in connecting me with God. However, I know that when I do that with the Lord's Prayer, I am missing out on how incredibly big and powerful it is. It is, in fact, the perfect framework to help us connect with Father God.

First, it points us to who he is, our Father in heaven, speaking of closeness and intimacy with the Father but also of his greatness. Then, the focus is on his kingdom. His kingdom is big, and it is here. His kingdom is perfect; other kingdoms rise and fall, but God's does not. Next, we ask for our basic needs. We ask him to provide us with what we need, to fuel us to do his work. Forgiveness follows. We are fed and forgiven, so we need to go on and do the same.

When we pray the Lord's Prayer, we realign our hearts with God's heart and we ask him to draw closer to us as we draw close to him.

Take a few moments to read the Lord's Prayer and then pray it, taking time to consider each part as you read it.

ANNIE WILLMOT

Don't worry

'Look at the birds of the air; they do not sow or reap or store away in barns, and yet your heavenly Father feeds them. Are you not much more valuable than they? Can any one of you by worrying add a single hour to your life?' (NIV)

When I was a child, I would often get tummy aches and feel dizzy because I'd get so worked up going over and over things in my mind. I worried about friendships, about doing something that would get me into trouble, about not doing well at school, about my appearance, about being bullied. Anything that could be worried about, I did.

When I read this verse, I think of my mum. As an adult, I've learned a lot from her about not worrying – a lot of which I wish I'd learned as a child!

She told me recently about some conversations she'd had with friends after discussing fairly big things that were happening. Once, after requesting prayer, she was asked, 'How can you sleep at night for worrying?' She replied, 'I don't worry. What's the point?'

And then someone asked, 'But don't you care?' She responded, 'Of course I care, but I would make myself ill if I worried about it all.'

She chooses instead to put her trust in God and his promises.

I became completely overwhelmed with worry at university. All of a sudden, I realised it wasn't sustainable and that it was really damaging my health. I knew I needed to choose instead to trust in God.

Jesus doesn't say that it's easy not to worry, but he tells us to seek God's kingdom first and the rest will follow. He makes it clear that worrying really will do nothing to help us!

Worrying isn't something you can just stop. It gets a hold of us. It takes a conscious choice to keep putting down the worry and keep trusting in God, but the more we do it the more our attitudes are changed.

Take a moment to reaffirm your trust in God and his promises and give him all of the things you might be inclined to worry about today.

ANNIE WILLMOT

Don't judge

'You hypocrite, first take the plank out of your own eye, and then you will see clearly to remove the speck from your brother's eye.' (NIV)

Jesus calls us not to judge others, but this can feel pretty tricky in a world where it seems we're constantly invited to judge. When we watch shows like *Britain's Got Talent* or *Strictly Come Dancing*, or when we watch the news and make decisions about situations and people based on limited information, or when we're in conversations that turn to gossip, we're judging, judging and judging again.

I know I'm as quick to judge as everyone else. If someone 'steals' the parking space I've been waiting for, or cuts in front of me in a queue, I jump to judgement. I have no idea what's going on for that person and certainly know nothing about their heart; I have no idea what kind of day they're having or anything about their lives. I know I wouldn't want someone to judge me in that way.

I love imagining the ridiculousness of trying to help someone remove a speck from their eye while you've got a whacking great piece of wood in yours! When Jesus tells us to take our plank out first before we can help another remove her speck, he's telling us to be accountable to him for our own sins before pointing out someone else's.

In this passage Jesus calls us not to judgement but to *discernment*. We can't know other people's hearts as he does, but in Christian community and fellowship we grow in mutual understanding and can help each other come closer to God.

Once we allow God to remove those self-satisfied planks out of our own eyes, we can see more clearly where he is at work, and can help others to do the same.

Spend a moment asking God to help you to remove any wrong judgement from your heart and for him to use you to help others draw close to him today.

ANNIE WILLMOT

Do ask, seek and knock

'Ask and it will be given to you; seek and you will find; knock and the door will be opened to you. For everyone who asks receives; the one who seeks finds; and to the one who knocks, the door will be opened.' (NIV)

Ask, seek, knock: three actions which seem so simple, but they're not a one-time instruction.

Jesus is telling us to pray, and keep praying: to keep asking, to keep seeking the kingdom of God and to keep knocking. He encourages us to be both persistent and active. Asking with our mouths, seeking with our minds and moving into action by knocking. Over and over again, the Bible makes it clear that following Jesus isn't something we can do passively.

He invites us into relationship and promises that when we seek him we will find him and be changed. The persistence he's calling us to isn't like that of a child who desperately wants something and keeps asking over and over again, not listening to or understanding why they can't have it. Instead, it's a persistence that keeps asking God to know him more and to know his will.

It's important that we do all three: ask, seek, knock. When we seek God, our hearts become more like his and we find we're asking for things on his heart too. When we knock on the door and enter into relationship with him, we learn to listen and find that sometimes he says 'yes', sometimes 'no', sometimes 'not yet'. However, we keep on praying.

I remember once hearing a deeply encouraging and challenging story of a preacher who prayed for many years for specific people to come to know God. When he died, he hadn't seen all the people on his list come to faith – but at his funeral, the last four did.

Asking, seeking and knocking is a lifelong thing. We may not always get to see the thing we've been persistent for, but that doesn't mean we stop. God is always at work, even when we don't see it.

Are there things or people that you've stopped praying for? Spend some time asking, seeking and knocking as you bring that thing or person before God again today.

ANNIE WILLMOT

Do be amazed

When Jesus had finished saying these things, the crowds were amazed at his teaching, because he taught as one who had authority, and not as their teachers of the law. (NIV)

Imagine the scene: the crowds are sitting at Jesus' feet. He finishes speaking and perhaps some of them turn to one another and chat about what they've just heard; perhaps others just sit there, speechless. They are amazed at his teaching and his authority.

I wonder, when we hear Jesus' teaching, are we amazed? I know sometimes I skim over passages in my Bible because I think I know them, or I only half listen to a sermon. I don't even give myself an opportunity to be amazed. The word of God is powerful and authoritative, but sometimes we don't treat it that way.

I love listening to my three-year-old talk about the gospel with excitement and demonstrate a need to tell others. Recently, we were in a soft play centre. He was playing with another child and I overheard him telling her the gospel story, in great detail. Rather than listening and thinking, 'Wow, it's amazing to hear him share that with such authority and passion', I thought, 'Uh oh, I think her granny is listening. Where is this going to go?'

That same authority that Jesus taught with is the authority he gave the disciples, and he gives to us. We have that full authority to go out and share his word. Do we believe it? My son certainly does.

I want to hear the Bible with the same amazement he hears with, and I want to hear it like that over and over again. And I want to share it with others with that sense of amazement, with the authority that Jesus has given me. If you read on in Matthew, you'll see numerous signs and wonders all performed in Jesus' authority. That's what I want to expect to see because I know that same power is at work in me.

Ask God to speak to you today as you read his word. Take some time to be amazed today.

ANNIE WILLMOT

Family ups and downs: Isaac and sons

Sheila Jacobs writes:

If any family had ups and downs, it was certainly this one! Abraham's immediate descendants are no plaster saints; they sometimes act in the most appalling manner. But what really strikes me is that, although they are clearly just imperfect human beings, as we all are, our good, faithful, patient God is at work in their lives. He doesn't turn away from them because they get it wrong. Far from it. He has a plan.

If ever we can see that our eyes should be on God and not on people, it is through the story of Isaac and his sons. Isaac, the special child, the one long-awaited by Abraham, is deceived by his wife and by the younger son who is her favourite, not his. His elder son, Esau, seems to despise his own birthright and gives it away for a bowl of stew. And then there's the manipulative Jacob, renamed 'Israel', the one who struggles with God, in the life-changing encounter with a mysterious 'man' in what seems to be a divine wrestling match. Jacob, whose original name essentially means 'supplanter' – it suited him well – is given his new name by God. (Maybe you need to know that God has 'renamed' you, too.)

I don't know what your family situation, or your church family, is like. Our relationships in general may – and do – have their issues, but be encouraged that God doesn't pick perfect people and families. You'll find no ancient heroes in these passages – there is, in fact, only one hero, and that is God himself. Be prepared to be astounded as you read afresh of his grace and goodness in the lives of ordinary people. Are you flawed and imperfect? Join the club. Are you struggling and needing breakthrough? Look to God.

This isn't a study in how to deal well with difficult family circumstances, but hopefully it will inspire you to look beyond any immediate problems and remember that just as our loving God had a good plan for those who lived long ago, he has a plan for you and for me. And he *never* gives up on us!

Show me, Lord

'I want you to swear by the Lord, the God of heaven and the God of earth, that you will not get a wife for my son from the daughters of the Canaanites, among whom I am living.' (NIV)

Families come in all shapes and sizes. But a good, stable marriage, lifelong fidelity and love are God's idea. Here, we see Abraham looking out for his son, thinking about his future. Yes, Isaac needs a wife; but not just anyone will do.

By engaging his servant to find his son the right woman, Abraham elects to send him to his own relations, his own kin. Today, we might equate this with looking for a marriage partner who believes as we do, has the same Father – God. Apart from the fact that there are scriptures that challenge us on unequal yoking (2 Corinthians 6:14; see also 1 Corinthians 7:39), why try to establish a lifelong union with someone who doesn't see the most important thing the same way we do? Easy to say, of course, but not quite so easy to put into practice. As a lifelong single, I know that we may often be tempted to take matters into our own hands and look outside of what we know to be God's perfect will.

Here, I love how the servant puts the whole issue into God's hands. Is this the right person? Show me, Lord. And if it isn't…?

Do we trust God enough, that he is reliable? That he has a perfect plan for us? That he cares about us, and knows what we need? That while we can't see the future, he can? Good friends are invaluable; we should listen to godly counsel in the area of relationships. But first and foremost, let's ask God, trusting him to direct us. And leave in his hands the outcome of whatever we are seeking him for.

If you're hoping to meet someone, or perhaps are in a relationship that isn't working (or know someone in this position), bring it all to God. He knows. He cares. Trust him to show you his will.

SHEILA JACOBS

I will go

He said to them, 'Do not detain me, now that the Lord has granted success…' Then they said, 'Let's call the young woman and ask her about it.' So they called Rebekah and asked her, 'Will you go with this man?' 'I will go,' she said. (NIV)

Picture this. Young Rebekah meets a stranger by a well. He asks her for a drink and she generously offers to water his camels as well. The next minute, she discovers she is the answer to his prayers. It turns out that her family and that of his master are kin. Then her brother gets involved, and before she knows it, she is being asked to go with this stranger to marry a man she has never met. And she says yes.

There seems to be no fear in Rebekah. Perhaps the privilege and excitement of being chosen and lavished with presents have taken the edge off any natural reluctance. Or maybe she just *knows* this is something of God.

When God asks us to 'step out of the boat', it can be exciting but frightening too. Many of us don't like change, and while the idea of adventure sounds thrilling, when it comes down to it, our comfort zone seems a pretty good place to be. I was challenged recently about this very thing. Had I become so comfortable that I had forgotten that this life isn't about my comfort; it is about the outworking of a plan that God has for me?

If you're like me, you get excited by the thought of taking a risk for God, but when it comes to actually *doing* it, all the reasons why it may not be a good idea come flooding in. Safer to stay at home. Stay with what you know… it's not too bad where you are, is it? You might be walking into something difficult. Don't rock the boat!

Perhaps sometimes we need the courage to say, with Rebekah, 'I will go', and see what God will do.

Is God is asking you to step out in faith in a certain area? What's stopping you? Talk to God about this now, bringing your fears and concerns and asking him to replace them with his peace.

SHEILA JACOBS

United in grief

Then Abraham breathed his last and died at a good old age, an old man and full of years… His sons Isaac and Ishmael buried him in the cave of Machpelah near Mamre… There Abraham was buried with his wife Sarah. (NIV)

After Abraham's wife Sarah died, he marries again – we read of his concubines and his many offspring. Without getting into the whole issue of sexual morality here, Abraham seems fully aware that of all his children, only one is the child of promise – Isaac. Abraham leaves him everything he owns and sends his other sons away.

His first child, Ishmael, has also been sent away from his father, as we can read earlier. Ishmael, you may remember, is the child of the slave woman – born of Abraham and Sarah's attempt to outwork God's promise themselves, rather than let God be God. It led to much suffering and strife for all concerned and a great deal of understandable tension between the boys (Genesis 21:8–10). Ishmael probably felt utterly displaced in his father's affections by his younger half-sibling. We can only imagine the natural, human rejection he must have struggled with.

One of the issues with step-families, I think, is the tensions which can occur when there is a 'first family' and a 'second family' or a blended mix of step-siblings. It's a minefield of emotion, and to say it needs careful and sensitive handling is an understatement.

It's heartening to see that Isaac and Ishmael together bury their father. Grief can unite, as well as divide, families. The sad event of saying goodbye to Abraham shows something deeply significant: the great love that both boys had for their dad. Is it a reconciliation of sorts? More likely, it is a brief moment when old hurts are put aside as less than important in the overall scheme of things, a recognition of something greater than individual jealousies and rivalries – that life is short, and we need to live it in light of eternity.

Is there someone you need to make it up with? Or a situation you know you should let go of? Do it now. Or share and pray with a trusted friend.

SHEILA JACOBS

117

Differences

The boys grew up, and Esau became a skilful hunter, a man of the open country, while Jacob was content to stay at home among the tents. Isaac, who had a taste for wild game, loved Esau, but Rebekah loved Jacob. (NIV)

It is fascinating to see the differences in siblings. An older brother might be a quiet introvert, their younger sister a fiery extrovert. And of course, one child may prefer to spend time with dad, while the other is more like mum in temperament. That seems to be what we are reading about here in the relationship between Esau and Jacob and their parents.

Sadly, there seems to be considerable favouritism – as becomes all too evident later. But, for all his father's favour, Esau appears to be a man of little integrity. He sells his birthright to his brother because he's hungry. His birthright – his position within the family, the firstborn's rights of inheritance – all for a bowl of stew! This episode doesn't show Jacob in a favourable light either. He's trying to manipulate his way to the top. This is clearly not a harmonious family, living together in unity. Is this speaking to us as a church family?

There will always be the laid-back and the go-getters. While it may be good to take a more relaxed view of the world, if that's our nature, let's not become careless. We need to value that which has been entrusted to us. Have some of us been believers for so long that we are taking our faith, our God, for granted?

Alternatively, the ambitious among us may try to do things 'our way'. I recall many years ago God saying that he didn't want me to work *for* him, but he wanted to do *his* work in and through me. We need to remember it is ultimately *God* who blesses. No scheming allowed in God's kingdom! And let's be wary of favouritism. Jesus wants unity among his followers (John 15:12), not warring factions.

Is there a sense of unhealthy competition in your home or your church? Gather together some people to pray for peace and an agreement to love, even while holding different views.

SHEILA JACOBS

Devious!

Now Rebekah was listening as Isaac spoke to his son Esau… Rebekah said to her son Jacob… 'Listen carefully and do what I tell you… so that he may give you his blessing before he dies.' (NIV)

If we're wondering where Jacob's scheming nature came from, I think this passage may give us a clue! It's quite shocking to think that Rebekah, chosen by God to be Isaac's wife, would deceive her husband in this way. Jacob has been trying to work things out for his own good. And now his mother is assisting him – in fact, this deception is her idea. Old and infirm, Isaac is about to be tricked into thinking the younger son is the elder. And so the blessing usually conferred on the oldest son will instead be given to Jacob.

Later, King David would wait for God to put him into a position of authority, as promised (see for example 1 Samuel 26). Here, Jacob wants what he wants; instead of refusing to go along with Rebekah's plan, he happily plays along. And yet he didn't need to hurt his father and brother to get where God wanted him to be.

It hardly needs saying that ruthless ambition is out of place in the Christian walk. But sometimes we can still 'step on others' to get where we want to be, even if we do it in subtle ways. We may want a particular position in the church, but we know someone else will get the job. Do we give way graciously or allow resentment to build up, leading perhaps to gossip, criticism and backbiting? How easy is it to take a back seat and wait? Can we be lovingly supportive to the person who has what we think should be ours and leave the rest to God? After all, isn't it all about Jesus – for his glory? And all about his kingdom?

Living in grace isn't easy. Letting God order our steps can be a huge act of humility and willing surrender.

Lord, please help me to fix my eyes on you and surrender to your will for my life. I know you love me. I trust your promises, and I give you all the glory. Thank you!

SHEILA JACOBS

Grudges

Esau held a grudge against Jacob because of the blessing his father had given him. He said to himself, 'The days of mourning for my father are near; then I will kill my brother Jacob.' (NIV)

Deceived twice by his brother, it is no surprise that Esau holds a grudge against Jacob. Esau just doesn't seem to be able to get it right; he marries the wrong women, and his parents clearly don't want Jacob to do the same thing. It seems expedient for Jacob to be sent to his mother's family to find a wife from among her brother's daughters – and it will also remove him from any potential trouble with Esau, who is so angry about being duped that his mother warns Jacob that his life is in danger.

Esau, it seems, tries to curry favour by marrying one of Ishmael's daughters. It appears he didn't realise how much his previous choice of wives had displeased his parents. I wonder why. Was he too busy pleasing himself to notice?

Esau's life seems a mess, doesn't it? A slide downwards with wrong choices, lack of communication, carelessness, alienation, a lack of discernment, then fury about how things have turned out.

It's so easy to blame others when things go wrong. And maybe sometimes other people really are at fault. Sadly, some hurts are never put right, and grudges can be held for a lifetime. Maybe you know a family like that – or even hurt members of a church, still holding on to resentment about something that happened years ago. Do you have unforgiveness towards someone?

We can't move forward while our eyes are fixed to a past event or person. It isn't about letting them off the hook; it's about letting *yourself* off that hook of bitterness. Jesus wants us to live free. Is it time to let go of past mistakes, blame, anger? Forgiving others isn't easy – and neither is forgiving ourselves. But it's a choice. Do you want to be free?

Spend some time thinking about the condition of your heart. Are you holding a grudge? Harbouring resentment? Unable to forgive – yourself, or others? Tell Jesus about it and ask him to set you free.

SHEILA JACOBS

He's with you!

When Jacob awoke from his sleep, he thought, 'Surely the Lord is in this place, and I was not aware of it.' (NIV)

Fleeing from his brother's wrath, using the excuse – although quite valid – of seeking a wife from among his mother's family, Jacob has his famous dream of the stairway to heaven, with angels ascending and descending on it and the Lord above it.

Up to this point, Jacob has hardly seemed the religious type. Far from it: he is an ambitious, manipulative deceiver. And yet here is God, making promises about Jacob's future blessings! God speaks of how he will watch over him and bring him back to the land he is leaving. The fact is, God is good, and he loves the unlovable. He is looking for people who want *him*, and that isn't dependent on how 'good' we think we are. Perhaps the most effective people in the kingdom are those who know they've messed up, and realise they need a Saviour. Some of us may be far from God when we encounter him. But nowhere is too far away for him to reach out and touch us.

I love the fact that Jacob says, 'God's here and I didn't know.' In dark times, when we may feel isolated from family and friends, we can often lose the sense of his presence: 'Where have you gone, Lord?' But he has promised never to leave or forsake us (Hebrews 13:5). Clouds cover the face of the sun, but it doesn't mean the sun isn't there.

When I had to put my mother, who had dementia, into a care home, I asked God why this had happened, and I received the answer: 'I'm in it with you.' God is faithful. He has never deserted me, and he won't desert you.

Jesus didn't promise that following him would be trouble-free (John 16:33). But we don't journey alone.

Are you feeling alone? Isolated? Troubled? God is with you, even if you don't feel his presence. Have confidence in him. Think of one thing to thank him for today, and then praise him.

SHEILA JACOBS

Feeling valued?

Jacob said to Laban, 'What is this you have done to me? I served you for Rachel, didn't I? Why have you deceived me?' (NIV)

The deceiver has been deceived! Finding his mother's brother, Laban, Jacob falls in love with one of his daughters and serves seven years for her. But then he discovers he has been tricked. He has married the older, less attractive sister, Leah.

Laban explains, somewhat belatedly, that the custom is to give the older daughter in marriage before the younger. Jacob can have them both, but he needed to marry Leah first. That's not part of the original deal, and Jacob feels cheated.

But what about Leah and Rachel? How does Rachel feel when the man she knows loves her spends the night with her sister? An enduring rivalry starts right there between the women.

We know that the women in that culture did not live with the kind of choices we have today, but Laban's dealings certainly lack sensitivity. Tricking Jacob into further service, he works things out for his own benefit. Did he ever wonder how his daughters might feel about the situation?

Sometimes choices are made in families and in church life that wound people. It's true that we can't please everybody all the time, and there may be good reasons for unpopular choices. But there is always a place for sensitivity – to make people feel as if they are valued and that their opinions count. Just listening to someone, spending time with them, can help them to know that they have worth. Taking time with someone in one-to-one prayer, inviting the Holy Spirit, can lead to a God-encounter.

Even today, not every woman in the world is in the privileged position of being able to choose who to marry or what career to pursue. Let's be grateful for the freedom we have.

How will you use the freedom God has given you?

Is there someone you can spend time with, one-on-one, to show them that you care? Perhaps you yourself would like to pray with someone, for God's leading and direction. Ask God for wisdom, and then arrange to meet.

SHEILA JACOBS

Rejection

When the Lord saw that Leah was not loved, he enabled her to conceive, but Rachel remained childless. Leah became pregnant and gave birth to a son… She said… 'Surely my husband will love me now.' (NIV)

Leah's story is one of rejection and of desperately trying to earn the love of someone who simply doesn't want her. Have you ever been in that position? Maybe it was a person you loved but the feelings weren't returned. Were you the child who always craved the love of a guardian, mum or dad who didn't seem able to give you the love you wanted or simply wasn't available? Perhaps you really wanted that promotion, but it was given to your colleague? Or a particular ministry, but someone else was chosen over you?

I think we've all known rejection of some sort in our lives, and there are probably those *we* have rejected too. Rejection can make us feel unworthy, unloved, not good enough. If we hold on to it, it can severely damage our self-image and blight our lives and our relationships.

The good news is, Jesus understands. He was rejected too (Isaiah 53:3), and he is the one who accepts us – he does not reject us. If you are feeling unloved today, remember that God so loved *you* that he sent his only Son so that you would not be separated from him, but have eternal life (John 3:16).

Just as Leah could not earn Jacob's love, however hard she tried, we cannot earn the love of God. All our religious works, going to church, being good will not make us right with him.

Ephesians 2:8 tells us that it is by grace – God's free, unearned favour – that we are saved, through faith; it isn't something we earn, it is a gift from God. A gift – not earned! All we have to do is receive it. Have you received the free gift of God's forgiveness?

Read Ephesians 2:8. Spend a few moments reflecting on that passage. Have you tried working to gain God's favour? Are you able to let go and rest in his love for you?

SHEILA JACOBS

Let it go!

When Rachel saw that she was not bearing Jacob any children, she became jealous of her sister. So she said to Jacob, 'Give me children, or I'll die!' (NIV)

Although our greatest sympathies in this story of two women married to one man may lie with the one who is so desperate to be loved, it is hard not to feel sorry for Rachel. She and her man are in love – and then her father gives her sister to her husband-to-be. She's got to share him with Leah, the first wife.

We can only begin to imagine the extent of the hurt feelings, jealousy and rivalry that must have existed, although the passage we are reading today gives us a clue.

Jealousy can be deeply corrosive, leading to bitterness that can colour our whole life. At its root, it is wanting something that belongs to someone else. It could be about a thwarted goal – we see someone with the nice house, the happy family, the great ministry, and we wonder why *they've* got it and we haven't. Or maybe we have lost something or somebody. Perhaps a significant other has walked away with someone new. Or we have had a lifelong rivalry with a sibling we believe has our parents' favour… oh, jealousy comes in many forms!

Whether we have suffered a loss that wasn't our fault or we are disappointed in life, can we decide today to *let it go*? Jealousy robs us of the peace, the joy of God's presence. Can we shift our focus from what we don't have, and fix our eyes on Jesus instead? That way, we can receive his strength and his rest. If we hold on to jealousy and resentment, we may miss what God may want to do in our lives right now, today – and the blessings he specially wants to give to us. Don't let jealousy steal another hour of your life!

Maybe like David in Psalm 142, you need to pour out your complaint before God. Know that he loves you; he understands. Turn it over to him and be confident that he has a plan for you.

SHEILA JACOBS

The driving seat

'My honesty will testify for me in the future, whenever you check on the wages you have paid me. Any goat in my possession that is not speckled or spotted, or any lamb that is not dark-coloured, will be considered stolen.' (NIV)

'My honesty.' Really? For all Laban's poor treatment of him, Jacob is hardly 'honest' with him. He immediately starts scamming his own father-in-law!

God has blessed Laban while Jacob has been with him; both men know it. But, of course, Jacob is forever trying to work out his own future. He's a schemer, but he doesn't have to be. God is with him!

Many of us have a real urge to try to 'make things happen' – in work, in family situations, and in church and our Christian lives. We might even believe God has promised us something, but it seems to be taking a long time, so we try to tweak events – give God a helping hand, so to speak. But trying to force God's hand isn't the way of peace; he has a particular plan for you and for me. He has already 'prepared in advance' the good things we will do (Ephesians 2:10). At times when it seems nothing is happening, he may be simply asking us to wait. We need to trust him: his will and his timing.

I'm constantly challenged about laying down my own agenda and being content with God's will. Recently I felt Jesus asking me to *follow him* as I contemplated my life. I saw a picture of a lake and a boat. I thought, 'I don't like boats; I'll make my own way to the other side of the lake – in a car.' I saw myself in this car, but weirdly, Jesus was in the passenger seat. The message was clear: 'You want to do things your way, I'll be with you. I promised to never leave you. But I won't be driving.'

It's as we allow Jesus to drive that we are blessed and can be a blessing to others.

Who's in the driving seat of your life? You? Or Jesus? Are you telling him which way you want to go? Is it time to let go of the wheel and trust him?

SHEILA JACOBS

The broken bits

Then the Lord said to Jacob, 'Go back to the land of your fathers and to your relatives, and I will be with you.' (NIV)

If life starts to feel a bit difficult, if people begin to change towards you, if things start to get awkward, what do you do? If you're Jacob, you run away.

True, Jacob was the instigator of much of his own trouble. He had deceived Laban just as he had deceived his brother, Esau. But here we see that when things got tough, Jacob resorted to old, learned patterns of behaviour. He fled.

Sometimes it's easier to cut and run than to deal with stuff – even in our own families and churches. But we need to be careful because, although we can run from situations and from people, there's one thing we can never leave behind – ourselves.

My family moved a lot when I was a child; consequently, I went to eight different schools. It could be a relief to leave behind old problems – the kids I may not have got along with, the lessons that I found too hard – and start fresh. But it had a knock-on effect. As a young adult, I found it easier to walk away than to stick with a difficult issue and see it through. I realised later that this was learned behaviour. Hopefully, I am a bit better at 'not fleeing' now.

It's interesting, though, that the Lord's plan was for Jacob to return to his homeland. It seems that God used the negative circumstances, the broken bits in Jacob's life, to bring about his ultimate plan.

We all mess up. We all get it wrong. But if we love God, he promises that he will work out everything for our good (Romans 8:28). God has a habit of bringing beauty out of broken situations – and people. Let's commit our way to him today and trust him with the broken bits.

Is there a situation that you are thinking of fleeing from? Have you asked God what his will is? Remember, he loves you and has a plan for your life.

SHEILA JACOBS

Wrestling with God

So Jacob was left alone, and a man wrestled with him till daybreak. When the man saw that he could not overpower him, he touched the socket of Jacob's hip so that his hip was wrenched as he wrestled with the man. (NIV)

In this passage, we see Jacob wrestling with a 'man' who, it appears, is the Lord himself.

Jacob, on his way back home, is clearly terrified at the thought of a family reunion with his brother, whom he has wronged. Esau is coming to meet him with several hundred men.

When life is ambling along, the urgency that has us crying out to God is often missing – if you're anything like me. It's often when we are in the direst of circumstances that we meet with God.

I recently had a crisis in my life, and it made me seriously seek God. I suppose in a sense I was wrestling with him. Wrestling in prayer isn't wrong, but there must be a time of knowing that God has heard us, then resting in that. Eventually the answer came in a picture of a boat (yes, another one!) on a shoreline. I felt the Lord say to me, 'I'm not asking you to row. And I'm not asking you to steer the course.' No. He just wanted me to be with him, and trust. Realising that he loves me, I knew I must let go of the situation and let him work it out.

Wrestling often happens when we want our own way: the self-life versus the Spirit-life. I think so much of Jacob's life reflects this whole battle.

Jacob walked with a limp after his encounter with God. In effect, he was humbled. He was different. He even had a new name. And so do we, as children of the King of kings; in fact, we have a whole new identity!

It's worth remembering, too, that sometimes humility paves the way back in broken relationships – in friendships, families and churches.

Are you wrestling? Or resting? Is it time to sit quietly before the Lord and listen out for that gentle whisper (see 1 Kings 19:12) that tells you of your true identity?

SHEILA JACOBS

Reconciled!

Jacob looked up and there was Esau... [He] bowed down to the ground seven times as he approached his brother. But Esau ran to meet Jacob and embraced him; he threw his arms around his neck and kissed him. And they wept. (NIV)

I love happy endings! Here we read of the brothers, Jacob and Esau, being reconciled. It's been quite a journey for Jacob, a journey which shows us that God never gives up on his imperfect people – or his good plan for our lives. We need to trust him and not strive. Striving can be like trying to make a piece of a jigsaw puzzle fit, when it was perhaps never meant to be there; it may even be part of someone else's puzzle.

We have already thought about reconciliation earlier in these notes (with Isaac and Ishmael), but now, as we perhaps review our own past, we may recall people who were once part of our 'puzzle' but are no longer around. Sometimes people slide out of our lives simply because seasons change. But at times there has been bad feeling and for some reason we have severed ties. Reconciliation isn't always possible, or wise, but can we pray for the people, family member or even the church concerned, asking God to help us?

To forgive, to walk together in love – even though we may disagree on many points – isn't always easy. As we have learned through looking at the lives of Abraham's family, we are all too human. So happy endings aren't always possible. But the good news is that, because of Jesus, as we trust in him our ultimate destination will indeed be a happy one. He has reconciled us to God (Romans 5:10), the greatest reconciliation of all. Because of him, we need not be separated from our Father God, but can spend eternity with him. Do you know him? Would you like to? Or perhaps you have travelled away from him. Is it time you came back?

Father God, thank you that you sent your Son so I can be reconciled with you. We need not be separated, because you have made a way for me to come back. Thank you, Jesus. Amen

SHEILA JACOBS

What does it mean to be wise? Proverbs

Caroline Fletcher writes:

Over the next nine days, we will be looking at just some of the many sayings in the book of Proverbs that talk about wisdom and foolishness.

Proverbs is an example of a literary genre known as wisdom literature. The books of Job and Ecclesiastes are other Old Testament books of this type. The first seven verses of Proverbs act as a preface and set out the purpose of the book. They tell us its aim is to help us attain wisdom, so we can lead a 'prudent' life and do 'what is right and just and fair' (1:3, NIV).

Today, many look down on faith as foolish, thinking humanity has advanced beyond religious beliefs. However, for the writer of Proverbs, wisdom cannot be separated from knowing and obeying God. 'The fear of the Lord is the beginning of knowledge' (1:7, NIV).

The book of Proverbs has a refreshingly wider definition of wisdom than is commonly held. It is not about academic intelligence or knowing a lot of information, even about God, but something that goes beyond head knowledge to encompass how we live and interact with others. Many of us will have come across very bright people who are not very pleasant. Because they do not treat others well, such people would not be considered wise according to Proverbs' definition. The book has a more holistic view: wisdom is within the reach of anyone who is willing to listen and follow advice, rather than being something only attainable by those considered traditionally clever.

The book of Proverbs is a compilation of several different collections of sayings. Many of them are short and pithy. What we need to be aware of is that these sayings often jump from one idea to another rather than always following a set theme throughout a chapter. It is best, then, not to read too many of them at once, so we can adequately take them in. As short pithy sayings, each one presents 'a slice of reality' (Roland E. Murphy, *Proverbs*, Thomas Nelson Publishers, 1998, p. xxvi), but they should always be compared with the rest of scripture and each other for a more complete understanding of God's ways.

Growing wiser

Then you will understand what is right and just and fair – every good path. For wisdom will enter your heart. (NIV)

What comes into your head when you hear the word 'wisdom'? Some wizened old character like the wizard Gandalf in J.R.R. Tolkien's *The Lord of the Rings*, perhaps? His brand of wisdom is too mysterious and unattainable to appeal to many! However, in Proverbs wisdom is something we should all seek, for it is about having insight from God to lead our lives in ways that are honouring to him. Verses 9–15 describe its benefits: wisdom guides us on to right paths, so we do not simply follow the crowd but can resist the pressure to live in ways that are not good for us or others.

So how do we become wise? Well, first we need to want wisdom. The writer talks of seeking it as enthusiastically as we would hidden treasure. This is easier said than done, though. We need to ask ourselves – do we really want to change our ways and do things differently? The verbs 'look' and 'search' in verse 4 imply effort is involved. We will need to pray and ask God for his insight into the everyday situations we face and not make decisions without asking for his guidance. We may need to seek out help with understanding the Bible, for example by finding a small group or course to go on. We may simply need to spend time in quiet when we pray, listening for those little promptings from God rather than, as I so often do, pouring out requests without giving God a chance to speak.

The encouraging thing the passage says is that 'the Lord gives wisdom'. Unlike an exam, where you can study hard but still fail, wisdom is an unmerited, free gift from God. If we are actively seeking to grow in God's wisdom, he will enable us to do that.

In what ways do you need wisdom in your life and what actions do you need to take to grow in it?

CAROLINE FLETCHER

The best way

Blessed are those who find wisdom, those who gain understanding, for she is more profitable than silver and yields better returns than gold. (NIV)

My son has recently completed the new harder GCSE exams, and so I am acutely aware that young people are under more pressure than ever over exam results. As a result, stress and mental health issues are on the rise. The message society seems to give our kids is that money is everything, so you must achieve good results in order to ensure you get a well-paid job.

Our passage presents a very different message: pursuing wealth ('gold', 'silver' and 'rubies') should not be our goal. We should be aiming for far better things: 'wisdom', 'understanding', 'sound judgement' and 'discretion'. And these are not qualities limited to academic people, but something we develop by walking closely with God.

However, following God's ways of wisdom can be hard. Taking different routes from those around us often involves courage. When my husband went into ordained ministry, we faced a difficult decision. We knew we would struggle to maintain the mortgage on the house we owned and would be living in a vicarage, and so, after prayer, we decided to sell our home. But that was not easy. We were so used to hearing the message that our security lies in material possessions that it was hard to trust God with our future financial needs.

If you feel God is guiding you to do something that goes against society's expectations and you need courage to take that step, be encouraged by what this passage says. Following God's wisdom will not always be trouble-free, but 'her paths are peace', 'her ways are pleasant' and 'she is a tree of life'. Also, the qualities you will develop by following God's wisdom will be 'an ornament to grace your neck' and so your true treasure.

What are your goals in life? Have you sought God's direction and his wisdom in your plans? Ask for his guidance and the courage to follow it.

CAROLINE FLETCHER

The truth within

The tongue of the righteous is choice silver, but the heart of the wicked is of little value. (NIV)

One of the issues Jesus had with the Pharisees was their belief that outward acts, such as ritual handwashing, could make them holy before God. He corrected this view – saying it is what comes out of a person that makes them unclean, not such external things (see Mark 7:18–23). This means it is words and actions that show how spiritual a person really is, because those things expose the character within.

The book of Proverbs echoes this with its emphasis on our words and what they reveal about what's inside us. Those who are wise will show this by what comes out of their mouths. The 'discerning' are made clear by their words of wisdom, and the righteous are revealed by a tongue of 'choice silver' and by speaking words that 'nourish many'. Fools, too, are exposed by their words: the 'mouth of a fool invites ruin' and 'spreads slander'.

What comes out of our mouths, then, reveals a lot about us. We can try controlling our tongues and watching what we say, but we can never completely cover up what is inside. When we are under pressure, the truth spills out, no matter how hard we try to contain it. I remember hearing a sermon illustration about this once. It said that we are like buckets of water filled to the top. When the bucket is completely still, the water stays inside. However, if it is picked up and jolted about, then water begins to spill out. Similarly, with the jolts of life, the real us tends to come out. Our insecurities, jealousies, grudges and so on are revealed in our words. What spills out when you are under pressure? And what does that reveal about the things that need to change inside you?

Rather than feeling downhearted about these imperfections, turn them over to God and ask him to transform you from within.

CAROLINE FLETCHER

Fools rush in

The way of fools seems right to them, but the wise listen to advice.
(NIV)

Verse 15 says that if we are wise, we will listen to advice and not be like fools who plough ahead, assuming they are always right. This reminds me of one of my favourite pieces of advice from Jesus, found in Luke 14:28–33. In this passage, he gives two illustrations which show the importance of taking time to think things through before acting. He describes someone wanting to build a tower who makes sure they have enough money before starting the building, so they are not left with the embarrassment of an unfinished project. He also describes a king who is thinking about going to war. This king takes time to consider whether he has a large enough army to face his opposition, so he is ensured a good chance of victory.

Our proverb and Jesus' words remind us that God expects us to use our brains and think through our plans before charging ahead. Often, however, in our enthusiasm to serve God, it is tempting to rush into projects and plans without taking the time to seek advice, prayerfully test our ideas and reflect on them carefully. The person who shouts loudly, 'Don't worry about the details; we can leave those to God' has not always got more faith than someone who asks difficult questions about plans and takes time to be convinced.

Of course, we also need to get advice from the right people, and we need to pray about the advice we receive to test whether it is from God. Listening to another's thoughts does not mean we should blindly follow their views; rather, we need to consider and test their words carefully. Who do we go to for advice? Are they wise and godly people?

Spend time reflecting and praying about any ideas and plans you are currently considering, and ask God for his wisdom and guidance.

CAROLINE FLETCHER

Fake news

The simple believe anything, but the prudent give thought to their steps. (NIV)

Verse 15 could have been written for the social media age: 'the simple believe anything'. We are always hearing about people being taken in by fake news. One ITV article, for instance, said that a false story claiming that the Pope backed Donald Trump for president was shared more than 960,000 times even though expressing support for particular politicians is not something popes are ever likely to do.

There is so much information available on the internet that it is not surprising it's becoming increasingly difficult for any of us to tell what is true and not to be misled. How many of us, for instance, feel down after looking at the rosy version of lives posted on Facebook and assume everybody else is having a much better time than us?

The second half of verse 15 gives us some wisdom not only on how to deal with the internet but also on coming to opinions and judgements in general. The prudent, it tells us, operate with caution and 'give thought to their steps'. Discovering the truth may, then, take some effort from us. For instance, how easy is it to rush into judging someone without taking time to find out the facts? How much effort do we put into discovering the truth about the issues facing our world, so we can speak in an informed way as Christians?

Verse 16 offers us some additional advice which is also very relevant to our social media age. It describes a fool as 'hot-headed', and some Bible versions add 'reckless'. This reminds me how shockingly common it is for people to respond to online posts with aggression and abuse. Let's remember our faith affects every area of our lives, even our online ones!

Dear Lord, help me, as Ephesians 6:14 says, to put on the belt of truth and know your wisdom in discerning what is true and in reaching opinions.

CAROLINE FLETCHER

Good communication

The tongue of the wise adorns knowledge, but the mouth of the fool gushes folly. (NIV)

The sense of the original Hebrew for this verse is that the wise make knowledge pleasant to hear. And when Proverbs talks about 'knowledge', it is not talking about general knowledge but about knowing God. So it is saying that the wise person can convey God's truth to others in a way that reveals its true beauty and relevance.

When I first became a Christian, in my teens, this was certainly not something I managed to do. I just blurted out to family that they needed to repent and then wondered why they weren't impressed! Indeed, a survey entitled 'Talking Jesus, Dig Deeper', which looked into how successful Christians are at sharing their faith, sadly revealed that 42% of adult respondents 'felt glad that they did not share the same faith' as a Christian who had spoken to them about the gospel (**talkingjesus.org/wp-content/uploads/2018/04/Talking-Jesus-dig-deeper.pdf**, p. 20).

So how can we be more effective in sharing the Christian message? As always, looking at how Jesus communicated must help. While we need to remember that Jesus was not popular with everyone, it is apparent that crowds flocked to hear his teaching. What made so many want to listen to him? Could it be because he explained things in ways people could understand and relate to? His parables, for instance, use illustrations from everyday life, and he also used humour such as in his warning to take the plank out of our own eyes before removing the speck from another's. And was it just his words? Jesus' compassion was obvious to all, especially those society looked down upon. What do you think we can learn from Jesus about communicating the gospel well?

Pray about any concerns you may have around presenting the Christian message effectively.

CAROLINE FLETCHER

True riches

By wisdom a house is built… through knowledge its rooms are filled with rare and beautiful treasures. (NIV)

Parts of the book of Proverbs have been used by some to support the so-called 'prosperity gospel', the idea that God always rewards faithful Christians with financial prosperity and material goods. Indeed, verses 3–4, which talk of wisdom establishing a house with rooms 'filled with rare and beautiful treasures', could be taken to suggest that God always rewards with wealth those who follow his ways. However, when we look at the Bible as a whole, we see that things are not so simple for those who follow God. Job, for instance, was a good man but lost all his wealth as well as most of his family, and Jesus taught that it is easier for a camel to pass through the eye of a needle than for a rich person to enter the kingdom of God.

The prosperity gospel may be an extreme view held by only a minority of Christians, but many of us can entertain something similar: the assumption that following God will make our lives trouble-free and protect us from all problems. How often, for instance, do we get annoyed with God when things are tough, even though he has never promised us an easy time?

So, if being a believer does not guarantee a life of wealth, health and permanent happiness, what kind of 'rare and beautiful treasures' can we be assured of as Christians? What would you list as the treasures all believers *can* know? For me, it would be God's guidance and strength in whatever faces us; joy in all circumstances; forgiveness and hope for the future; eternal life and God's transformation of us through the tough things we go through. The question I ask myself is – do I truly appreciate these godly treasures more than material possessions?

Spend time thanking God for the 'rare and beautiful treasures' that are yours through Christ.

CAROLINE FLETCHER

Criticism – friend or foe?

Like an earring of gold or an ornament of fine gold is the rebuke of a wise judge to a listening ear. (NIV)

There is much in today's verses about the positive power of words. A 'rightly given' word spoken is like precious gold set in silver, we are told. But apt words are not just encouraging ones; they can challenge, too, and we read that a wise 'rebuke' can be precious like gold to someone who is ready to listen. Loving others does not mean we never challenge them. Jesus himself rebuked the Pharisees and even his own disciples.

But how do we know when it is right to challenge someone? None of us wants to be judgemental or condemning, and so there are a lot of questions to consider first. Is our motivation good and do we genuinely care for the person concerned? Are our words spoken from love or out of frustration, anger or revenge? Are they words of wisdom or just our own opinion? Have we prayed first and asked for God's guidance or are we rushing in? Are we able to express our words with grace and love?

And how do we deal with criticism ourselves? It is something each of us faces in this world. Even Jesus himself was criticised, and not everything said, even when it comes from other Christians, is always helpful or correct. As Paul tells the Thessalonians, we need to 'test them all' to work out what is of God (1 Thessalonians 5:21). Revisiting these verses from Proverbs again will offer us some guidance here. First, it is a 'wise' person's rebuke that is described as precious: are those criticising us wise? Second, it is 'rightly given' words that are valuable: is there truth and validity in the criticism? If so, those words, while they might hurt at first, can end up being more valuable to us than gold.

Have you faced criticism recently or had to challenge someone? Bring to God your feelings over those things.

CAROLINE FLETCHER

No way out?

As a dog returns to its vomit, so fools repeat their folly. (NIV)

The image of a dog returning to its own vomit is pretty disgusting, but those of us who own dogs know it to be rather too true! Our canine friends will eat absolutely anything and never seem to learn from the experience. My Cavalier King Charles, for instance, loves nothing better than chewing underpants and eating horse manure!

Humans, too, can struggle to learn from past mistakes and get trapped repeating the same unhealthy behaviour over and over again. Indeed, the tragic flaw, the idea that some people have character traits which doom them to disaster, is central to much literature. For instance, the tragic flaw of Shakespeare's Macbeth was his ambition. It drove him on to repeat the same mistakes time and time again, murdering one person after another. Soap operas, too, are full of characters who get caught up in cycles of unhealthy behaviour: those who sabotage relationships again and again to protect themselves from getting hurt, for instance, or who, for self-esteem reasons, keep settling for the wrong kind of partner.

In Charles Dickens' *Bleak House*, there is a character called Harold Skimpole, who repeatedly scrounges off everyone else. His excuse is he cannot change; he is just a child in worldly matters.

The truth is all of us can change with God's help. With him there is no tragic flaw or doomed fate. God enables us to learn from the past rather than being defined by it. He can turn our mistakes, weaknesses and hurts into opportunities for growth and transformation, and bring us forgiveness, healing and hope. If we face our problems rather than bury them, and ask for God's help and that of other Christians, then we really can break free and make a fresh start.

As you come to the end of this issue of Day by Day with God, *spend a little time thanking God that he rescues, forgives, transforms and is always ready to give us a fresh start.*

CAROLINE FLETCHER

Enabling all ages to grow in faith

Anna Chaplaincy
Barnabas in Schools
Holy Habits
Living Faith
Messy Church
Parenting for Faith

The Bible Reading Fellowship (BRF) is a Christian charity that resources individuals and churches and provides a professional education service to primary schools.

Our vision is to enable people of all ages to grow in faith and understanding of the Bible and to see more people equipped to exercise their gifts in leadership and ministry.

To find out more about our ministries and programmes, visit

brf.org.uk

Recommended reading

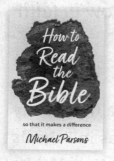

How to Read the Bible
... so that it makes a difference
Michael Parsons
978 0 85746 809 3 £8.99
brfonline.org.uk

To read and engage with the Bible, we first need to understand the story, the styles of writing and the approaches we find in the text. Michael Parsons encourages readers to look at the whole biblical storyline before demonstrating ways of approaching individual texts. Topics along the way include understanding different genres, the importance of narrative, imaginative reading, praying the Bible, difficult passages and what to do with them, and how to apply scripture to our own lives.

Praying the Way
with Matthew, Mark, Luke and John
Terry Hinks
978 0 85746 716 4 £10.99
brfonline.org.uk

Through raw and authentic prayers, based on the gospel stories, Terry Hinks leads readers into the heart of the gospels the more clearly to see the needs and joys of today's world. This highly original book helps readers to pray out of, and with, the words of Jesus and to discover the joy of prayer as a two-way conversation – listening as much as speaking to God.

To order

Online: **brfonline.org.uk**
Telephone: +44 (0)1865 319700
Mon–Fri 9.15–17.30

Delivery times within the UK are normally 15 working days. Prices are correct at the time of going to press but may change without prior notice.

Title	Price	Qty	Total
How to Read the Bible	£8.99		
Praying the Way	£10.99		
Day by Day with God (May–Aug 2020) – single copy	£4.70		
Day by Day with God (Sep–Dec 2020) – single copy	£4.70		

POSTAGE AND PACKING CHARGES			
Order value	UK	Europe	Rest of world
Under £7.00	£2.00	Available on request	Available on request
£7.00–£29.99	£3.00		
£30.00 and over	FREE		

Total value of books	
Postage and packing	
Total for this order	

Please complete in BLOCK CAPITALS

Title _____ First name/initials _____ Surname _____

Address _____

_____ Postcode _____

Acc. No. _____ Telephone _____

Email _____

Method of payment

☐ Cheque (made payable to BRF)   ☐ MasterCard / Visa credit / Visa debit

Card no. ☐☐☐☐ ☐☐☐☐ ☐☐☐☐ ☐☐☐☐ ☐☐☐☐

Expires end ☐☐ ☐☐   Security code* ☐☐☐   Last 3 digits on the reverse of the card

Signature* _____ Date _____ /_____ /_____

*ESSENTIAL IN ORDER TO PROCESS YOUR ORDER

Please return this form to:
BRF, 15 The Chambers, Vineyard, Abingdon OX14 3FE | enquiries@brf.org.uk
To read our terms and find out about cancelling your order, please visit **brfonline.org.uk/terms**.

The Bible Reading Fellowship (BRF) is a Registered Charity (233280)

Each issue of *Day by Day with God* is available from Christian bookshops everywhere. Copies may also be available through your church book agent or from the person who distributes Bible reading notes in your church.

Alternatively you may obtain *Day by Day with God* on subscription direct from the publishers. There are two kinds of subscription:

Individual subscriptions
covering 3 issues for 4 copies or less, payable in advance
(including postage & packing).

To order, please complete the details on page 144 and return with the appropriate payment to: BRF, 15 The Chambers, Vineyard, Abingdon OX14 3FE

You can also use the form on page 144 to order a gift subscription for a friend.

Group subscriptions
covering 3 issues for 5 copies or more, sent to one UK address (post free).

Please note that the annual billing period for group subscriptions runs from 1 May to 30 April.

To order, please complete the details on page 143 and return with the appropriate payment to: BRF, 15 The Chambers, Vineyard, Abingdon OX14 3FE

You will receive an invoice with the first issue of notes.

All our Bible reading notes can be ordered online by visiting
brfonline.org.uk/collections/subscriptions

Day by Day with God is also available as
an app for Android, iPhone and iPad
brfonline.org.uk/collections/apps

Follow us on Instagram: **@daybydaywithgod**

All subscription enquiries should be directed to:
BRF, 15 The Chambers, Vineyard, Abingdon OX14 3FE
+44 (0)1865 319700 | **enquiries@brf.org.uk**